The Use of

Academic Prediction Scales

for Counseling and Selecting

College Entrants

The Use of **ACADEMIC**

PREDICTION

SCALES

*for Counseling and Selecting
College Entrants*

Benjamin S. Bloom

and **Frank R. Peters**

The Free Press of Glencoe, Inc.

A DIVISION OF THE CROWELL-COLLIER PUBLISHING COMPANY

Foreword

THE MAIN THESIS OF THIS
report is that there are three sources of variation in academic
grades. One is the *errors in judgment* of teachers about the
quality of a student's academic achievement. Testers have
over-emphasized this source of variation and have tended to
view grades with great suspicion. Our work demonstrates
that this source of variation is not as great as has been
generally thought and that grade averages may have a
reliability as high as +.85, which is not very different from
the reliability figures for some of the best aptitude and
achievement tests.

Another source of variation in academic grades is the
difference among students in achievement and motivation.
This is the source of variation we attempt to measure as
directly as possible by means of tests and other evidence-

gathering procedures. Counselors and teachers assume this source of variation is represented in grades and in test scores and utilize this evidence for purposes of decision, prediction, and action. Although we have not treated this problem directly, the findings presented in this report make clear that high school teachers do make relatively precise judgments about students and that these judgments are highly related to judgments made by college teachers and to the results of achievement measures.

The third source of variation is the *difference in standards* from teacher to teacher and from school to school. It is the difference in standards from school to school (institutional variation) that we are studying and attempting to measure. Our research has succeeded in finding procedures for estimating this variation which permit a level of academic prediction that has been rare in educational research. Whether the methods described here are finally used or whether other more precise methods are developed in the future is not the central issue. The major point to be made is that the measurement of variation in standards results in a real breakthrough in academic prediction.

Much of this report is an attempt to make clear the variety of consequences that follow from this new level of precision in the prediction of academic achievement. Properly used, this new level of precision could greatly reduce academic failure in higher education. Properly interpreted, this new level of precision could have significant consequences for our testing methodology and educational research.

Perhaps the most important consequence for education is a renewed emphasis on the judgments made by teachers about student achievement. The proper use of grades can have far-reaching effects on academic motivation and work. However, teachers must do much to make these judgments more valid, more systematic, and more meaningful.

We are indebted to Mr. Cleveland A. Thomas, Director of the National Registration Office of the National Council of Independent Schools, and Mr. Francis Parkman, Executive Secretary of the National Council of Independent Schools, for the encouragement and support they gave to us and to the project. Mrs. Betty Hollander conducted a large number of pilot investigations that helped to determine the structure of the major study. Mr. Allen Herzog organized the enormous computational task and advised us on many of the statistical problems. We turned to Mr. Hugh Lane every time we got into difficulties. Mrs. Patricia Lawson typed the manuscript. Mrs. Eleanora Kauffman, Miss Shirley Golden, and Mrs. Mildred Lamoreaux had major shares in overcoming many of the difficulties we encountered in attempting to make sense out of an enormous mass of unwieldy data. We are grateful to all not only for the specific services they rendered but also for their cooperation and encouragement when our problem loomed so large.

This study was made possibly by the unusually fine collection of data represented in the Annual Reports of the National Registration Office for Independent Schools. The availability of the data on school and college grades of over 25,000 students in some 125 schools and about 600 colleges prompted us to seek the means of rearranging the pieces of this complex puzzle. The National Council of Independent Schools and the National Registration Office for Independent

Schools made this study possible by a grant for the research.

Since this study has made use of data collected for other purposes, we have been very careful to treat the identity of students, schools, and colleges as confidential. It is to be hoped, however, that the weight of the research evidence will induce schools and colleges to utilize similar methods and to report the necessary data to each other in order to maximize the educational values inherent in this country's secondary and higher educational institutions.

Contents

Tables

Charts

The Use of

Academic Prediction Scales

for Counseling and Selecting

College Entrants

1

Introduction

THIS STUDY WAS DESIGNED
to explore some methods by which the use of high school
grades for predictions of college success could be improved.
Estimates of the likelihood of college success are critical;
for from such estimates some high school graduates decide
to go to college and others decide not to, some young people
are admitted and other are denied. Such decisions have far-
reaching consequences for the individual, the schools and
colleges, and the nation. These consequences make it impera-
tive that we have good estimates, and good estimates can be
made only if we have good evidence. Our attempts to enhance
the usefulness of grades rests on the conviction that the best
available evidence of a student's academic capabilities and
achievements consists of the judgments made by the teachers
and professors who have worked with him over a period of
years.

3

This conviction rests on the principle that the best predictions of future behavior can be made from long and careful observation and analysis of relevant past behavior. In high school grades we have the summated reports of observations of the students' behavior over a three- or four-year span by many trained teachers in educational situations that approximate those likely to be encountered in college. Our conviction of the value of grades is also based on the fact that in the long history of attempts to improve predictions of college success, high school grades have consistently been found to be the best evidence from which to predict. Even so, predictions of college success are still notably inaccurate.

Attempts to improve predictions from high school grades have usually foundered because of variations in grading standards. These differences are not whimsical deviations of teachers and staffs. Schools and colleges serve different populations and have different problems, different programs, and different objectives. Within a school, such differences may be minimal, and the meaning of each grade may be relatively clear. When grades from a number of schools or colleges are compared the differences may be very great. The enormity of these differences is obscured by the fact that the schools and colleges use very similar grading symbols. Common sense tells us that an "A" grade from school X is not the same as an "A" grade from school Y, but awareness alone does not permit precise comparisons.

Insofar as differences in meaning of grades reflect differences in programs and objectives, such differences can be made clear only by careful analysis and contrast of the evidence used in arriving at grades. This we have not tried to do. We were concerned only with differences in the import of grades for prediction of later achievement in academic situations.

Our evidence clearly indicates that several methods can be used to adjust grades for prediction purposes, and each method will substantially increase the correlation between high school and college grades. With grade adjustments, the correlations reach the level of +.70 to +.80 in contrast with the usual level of about +.50. Some of our correlations for particular schools or colleges are as high as +.85. The results were remarkbaly stable over time, with different populations, and with different techniques. These results are impressive when they are compared with other prediction techniques, for correlations of this magnitude between college grades and other measures—aptitude tests, achievement tests, and personality and interest tests—have rarely been found. In fact, there is reason to believe that if Academic Prediction Scales are applied, it should be possible to approach the upper limits of prediction efficiency permitted by the reliability of the criterion—college grades.

In brief, research reported here makes it clear that errors of estimate can be greatly reduced, and advisement of students, choice of college, and college admissions can be substantially improved.

Where Do We Stand in Prediction?

The problem of predicting college success has probably received more public attention than any other single problem in education. The amount of effort, thought, time, and money that has been poured into attempts to improve academic prediction has been very great. Thousands of studies have been published, and these represent but a small fraction of those that have been made. The reasons for this intense interest are clear. In our society, the transition from school to college is one of the most critical choice points in the life of the individual. Up to this time the student has been more or less legislated through school. He may have had some choice of studies, some choice of curriculum, but for most high school graduates there is little choice of whether or not to attend school and no choice of which school to attend. At graduation, however, many alternatives become possible: to go to college or to get a job; to go to this college rather than one of a hundred others; to take this course rather than some other. The student may make his decisions alone, or he may decide on the basis of his parents' wishes, his high school counselors' advice, or on the basis of a friend's counsel or example. Whatever the grounds for his choice, he will be affected by the consequences of his decisions. If he chooses a course, a college, and a curriculum that fulfill his needs and that challenge but do not overtax his capabilities, he is likely to gain much from higher education. If he chooses a college and program with requirements far above his possibility of attainment, he will suffer the frustration and the loss of time and opportunity consequent on failure.

There will always be college failure, of course, for all educational endeavors are challenges, and to be challenged implies the possibility of failure. But errors stemming from gross underestimates or overestimates of a student's capabilities and potential achievements not only lead to failure, they preclude educational challenge in its best sense. The boy who is grossly incapable of understanding college algebra is not challenged by instruction in that subject, he is crushed by it. The boy who is capable and prepared to attack complex academic problems is not challenged by elementary instruction, he is bored. The problem in academic prediction is to prevent gross errors and to cut waste, so that real educational challenges can be offered and mastered.

The matter of choice is not just the student's concern, however, for teachers, parents, schools, and colleges are involved. Justly or unjustly, if the graduates of a school choose badly, if many of its graduates are college failures, the school will bear the wrath of parents and boards and the recriminations of colleges. Colleges that accept students who fail suffer great losses in utilization of faculty and other resources. With costs so high there is little wonder that numerous and repeated attempts to enhance predictions of college success are made.

In spite of the many studies which have been made in order to find accurate predictors of college success, little progress toward improved prediction has been noted. Current studies and reports reflect findings similar in level and precision to those of studies and reports made thirty or forty years ago. We have many more tests and larger and more effective centralized testing services and nationwide testing programs; there have been many modifications and innovations in statistical techniques and research designs; there have been improvements in the interpretations of grades and grade distributions; yet it is still unusual to find a correlation between college grades and other measures above the level of +.60, and most correlations reported fall in the range +.45 to +.55. For most colleges, the odds are still 50-50 or less that an entrant will graduate, i.e., for every 100 students admitted to college, 50 or more will drop out before graduation. (Iffert, 1956.)

Academic Predictors—Grades

The idea that one might avoid some of the gross errors in college selection and admission by interpreting the applicant's high school record is not new or different. In the United States, high school records have been the most widely used evidence for estimating college promise. In some instances this use is restricted merely to the determination that the college applicant is a high school graduate. But most often the student's grades and his course of studies are examined.

The extensive use of grades for prediction has warranted and received intensive study. As early as 1917, Lincoln (1917) reported a correlation of +.69 between high school standing and freshman college standing for 253 Harvard students who had reached junior or senior rank. In 1920, Jordan (1922) found a correlation of +.50 between high school senior grades and college freshman grades for a group of students at the University of Arkansas. In his review of the literature on college prediction studies up to 1933, Segel (1934) summarized the findings of twenty-three studies of the prediction of general college scholarship using average high school marks. The forty-eight coefficients cited ranged from +.29 to +.69, with a median value of +.55.

Since 1933 there have been hundreds of additional studies published on college prediction, and in these studies high school grades have almost always been included as a predictor. In fact, most researchers have come to the conclusion that high school average grades are the best single measure from which to predict college success. Odell (1927) reached this conclusion in 1927 as did Travers twenty years later. Travers (1949), who cited more than two hundred prediction studies in his review, concluded that average high school grades surpass either subject matter tests or psychological tests as predictors of college grades.

The fact that grades have been shown to be the best single evidence from which to predict college achievement does not alter the fact that the level and precision of predictions from grades have remained relatively low and stable. The College Board report for 1957 (Fishman, 1957), for example, cites fifteen correlations between high school marks and average freshman grades. The correlations cited range from +.30 to +.59, with a median value of +.41.

The Fallibility of Grades
as Predictors

It is not necessary to go into a lengthy analysis to discover why raw high school grades do not provide better predictors of college success than they do. There is an extensive literature on the variability of grading standards and the unreliability of grades. Such differences can be traced partly to the variations mentioned before among schools in purposes and programs, partly to differences in the levels of expectations of teachers and faculties, and partly to differences in the general aptitude of students. Chauncey and Frederiksen (1951), for example, pointed out that "a high-ranking student in a school whose pupils have an average I.Q. of 125 is likely to be more able than a high-ranking student in a school whose pupils have an average I.Q. of 95." Equally important reasons for variability in the meaning of grades stem from differences in the purposes of teachers and in the traits or qualities which are considered in the assignment of grades. Within the same subject matter area, there often are wide divergencies of programs and purposes among different colleges. Dressel and Mayhew (1954), for example, have pointed out some of the important differences in the general education programs of different colleges.

It is common knowledge that some schools have programs in which the emphasis is on preparation for college while other schools have curricula designed as technical or terminal.

The Eight-Year Study (Aikin, 1942) highlighted fundamental differences among schools in the courses of study and methods of instruction, with some schools largely dedicated to the classical forms and other schools aiming toward reorganized subject matter and "problem" approaches. By and large, all of these differences are submerged when similar grading symbols are used. An "A" in English may signify that the student has demonstrated a clear and concise writing ability, or it may signify that he has mastered the rules and principles of mechanics, grammar, and syntax. Although these are not distinct achievements, they are not necessarily identical. Consequently, one cannot assume that two "A's" are identical in import. It is no wonder, then, that predictions based on the assumption that similar marks or ranks denote equivalent achievement are less effective than we would like.

The fact that such differences as the foregoing exist, however, is not cause for attacking the grading system as bad or ineffective. Grades are used for many purposes other than prediction of college success. For some purposes it is extremely important that grades reflect local educational objectives, standards, and norms even though such restriction adversely affects the usefulness of grades for prediction in other situations. Grades are used to inform students how well they are doing. Clearly the student will better understand this information if he knows the local standards and the criteria on which it is based. If someone is told that he writes a little better than most of his friends and acquaintances, he will probably understand more clearly what this means than if he is told that he writes a little better than the average American adult male. What we are attempting to demonstrate

in this report is that adjustments can be made that will
generally give the student and the college better information
about college potential without infringing on the use of grades
for other equally important purposes.

Techniques for Improving
Predictions from Grades

Attempts to modify or adjust grades in order to improve
college predictions are not new. Most admissions officers and
high school counselors judge a student's record in the light
of their appraisal of different schools and colleges. A student
who has an "A" record from Harvard or Yale, for example,
will usually be judged more able than a student with an "A"
record from any of a number of state universities. And, rightly
or wrongly, a student with a "C" record from a school whose
students ordinarily go on to college and do well will often
be more favorably viewed as a college risk than a "C"
student from a school whose students have a poor record in
college. There is great difficulty in determining the accuracy
of such appraisals; accuracy is obviously limited since it is
difficult to know many schools well and to keep account of
changes in students and school programs.

Other systematic attempts to take account of variability in
grading systems have been suggested and tried. The most
widely used technique is rank-in-class rather than average
grades. A number of studies have shown that this procedure
will slightly increase the correlation between high school

record and college marks. The use of rank-in-class rather than average grades is a statistical device for discounting differences in grades distributions. That is, if in one school 30 per cent of the students have a "B" average or better and in another school only 10 per cent have a "B" average or better, the use of rank-in-class will remove this apparent discrepancy in the proportions of high grades given. The assumption is that for prediction we should expect equivalent distributions of academic potential among student bodies. This assumption is not necessarily tenable in many comparisons, of course, for there are schools where only a small proportion of the students are potential college material, while a large proportion of the students from another school may be good college risks. The use of rank-in-class accounts for differences in grade distribution but does not reduce, and may magnify, errors due to differences in the level of instruction or the general ability of the students.

Another systematic effort to improve predictions of college success from high school grades involves a codification and extension of the use of experience records. Chauncey and Frederiksen (1951, p. 88), for example, reported that at Princeton and Yale studies have been made of every school sending large numbers of students to these universities. Corrections in rank-in-class estimates were made on the basis of the achievement of these former students from different schools. Chauncey and Frederiksen reported that rank-in-class corrected for a specific school or type of school tended to correlate with freshman grades at the +.60 level. Although such procedures may significantly increase correlations, the method is inherently limited in applicability and is costly. It is applicable only to situations where a limited number of schools send substantial numbers of graduates to a single college, and in such cases the students from other schools cannot be included. For example, Burnham (1959) found a correlation of $+.76$ between adjusted school grades and Yale freshman averages for students from schools that had sent several candidates to Yale over a period of years. However, this population constituted only a fraction of Yale students. Where only limited data were available from the schools the correlation between high school grades and Yale grades was only $+.42$. This limitation is likely to become more serious in the future since the composition of college groups is becoming more diversified. Colleges are increasingly drawing students from wider geographic areas. Even though a college keeps extensive records, it is likely to have more and more students from schools previously unrepresented in that college or at best represented by only a small number of students. In such cases, the college would have little basis on which to adjust an applicant's grades.

Use of experience records was greatly enhanced by the creation in 1945 of the National Registration Office for Independent Schools by the National Council of Independent Schools. The National Registration Office prepares an annual report that lists the high school records and freshman college grades of students from over one hundred member schools. Students are included from the previous five-year period. Admissions officers and school counselors who would otherwise have to rely on experience with only their own students are thus able to use the experience of a large number of colleges and schools.

An admissions officer may use this report in several ways in order to obtain a better estimate of a student's potential. He may simply consider all colleges as equal challenges and thus obtain a total picture of the college success of a particular school's students, or he may on the basis of his own judgment consider the records of only those students in colleges with standards which he believes to be similar to those of his own college. It is possible, too, for the admissions officer to obtain some check on his own judgment of the equivalence or non-equivalence of a college's standards by analyzing the records of students from schools that are represented in both his own college and the college in question. Thus, if school X had sent twenty "B" students to one college and twenty "B" students to another, a rough estimate of the equivalence of the two colleges in terms of grading standards could be obtained by comparing the college records of these two groups of students.

The report was revised in 1955 in order to make possible a more systematic summary of the college grades of each school's students. The colleges were grouped into three types on the basis of an analysis of all the N.R.O. records of the students who had attended each college. Type I included colleges where students from member schools had earned freshman average grades that were higher than the average grades they had received in secondary school; Type II included colleges where the average college freshman grades were about the same as the average grades the students had received in school; and in Type III colleges the average freshman grades were lower than the grades the students had received in school. The report then grouped the records of students from each school into the three types of colleges attended. Each college was advised as to the type in which it was placed. Consequently, a college admissions officer could use for analysis of a student's grade the summated records of other students from that school who had attended colleges included in the same type. The report is still limited by the relatively small number of schools involved. Nonetheless it represents a major step in improving estimates of college success from high school grades.

Another approach to the problem of differences in the import of grades for prediction involves the use of test data as the basis for adjustment. Toops (1933) suggested a method for the "transmutation of marks" that would reflect differences in the intelligence level of student populations. He argued that for purposes of prediction the two most important reasons why grades are non-comparable are that grade distributions vary and that the intelligence distributions of the pupils may not be equal. He suggested that "the average marks of all pupils of a given narrow range of intelligence in each of two schools are equal no matter if the two average marks are of different magnitude and are couched in different marking systems."

In order to correct for differences in intelligence level, Toops presented a regression technique by which grades of students of equal intelligence from different schools would be made equivalent. For example, if students in school I who made grade averages of "B" had intelligence test scores ranging from the 80th to 90th percentile and if students in school II who made grade averages of "C" had intelligence test scores ranging from the 80th to 90th percentile, then the "B"

grade in school I would be made equivalent to the "C" grade
in school II. Toops' method is essentially the same as the
Aptitude Method we describe in Chapter 2.

Reitz (1934) did make use of scholastic aptitude scores
to adjust the grades of students entering the University of
Chicago. These adjustments to the grades of individual students (not to the schools) did improve the prediction of
college grades. Aptitude scores were used at Muskingum
College (Muskingum College Faculty, 1937) as a basis for
re-examining grading practices.

In Great Britain, similar methods were investigated in a
major study of the secondary school placement of primary
school students. McClelland (1942) and his associates set
out to find the relative predictive values of intelligence and
scholastic tests, teachers' estimates, and ordinary (qualifying)
examinations and to determine the best combinations of these
measures for selecting pupils for secondary courses. They
found that teachers' marks tended to overestimate weak pupils
and underestimate top students and that standards varied
considerably from school to school. The last difference was
of greatest concern, for it precluded maximum predictive
efficiency. To correct for differences in standards, the authors
transformed teachers' marks on the basis of the mean and
standard deviation of the scores made by the pupils of the
various schools on a uniform test or examination in the same
subject. In short, an achievement test was used to establish
the relative standing of each school, and marks were adjusted
accordingly.

Barn and McClelland found that scaling teachers' marks
in the manner described consistently yielded higher correla-

tions between measures of secondary school success and
primary teachers' marks. In Table I, correlations of various
indices with average marks in different types of secondary
schools are shown.

Table 1—Correlations Between First-Year Average Marks in Secondary Schools and Various Predictive Indices *

Correlation with	Senior Secondary School	Boys' Technical Course	Girls' Technical Course	Commercial Course
Intelligence Test Score	.71	.62	.63	.53
Intelligence Quotient	.69	.60	.61	.52
Scholastic Test—English	.60	.52	.51	.46
Scholastic Test—Arithmetic	.69	.47	.57	.51
Qualifying Examination—English	.75	.63	.60	.60
Qualifying Examination—Arithmetic	.69	.50	.53	.49
Primary Teachers' Marks	.66	.58	.60	.53
Scaled Teachers' Marks	.74	.66	.64	.64
No. of Students	368	768	541	342

* Adapted from McClelland (1942, pp. 65, 71)

Contrast of the last two rows in Table 1 illustrates the increase
in correlations yielded by scaling primary teachers' marks.
McClelland (1942) reported that scaled marks improved
prediction not only in final combined results, but for every
senior secondary school and for every year.

In a later study of the placement of primary school leavers
in secondary schools in England, Yates and Pidgeon (1957)
used McClelland's research as a basis for correcting teachers'
estimates of the probable success of students in secondary
courses. They found that primary teachers' assessments scaled
by their method were the best single predictors of secondary
school achievement and that the superiority of the scaled

assessments over all tests used and other assessments was statistically significant.

Academic Predictors—
Aptitude Test Scores

Since the 1920's, aptitude tests have been widely used to predict college achievement. The testing of aptitudes was initiated under Wundt and the German psychologists and in its first stages was restricted to measuring such things as hand grip, reaction time, etc. Cattell brought a number of these tests to Columbia at the end of the nineteenth century and soon thereafter Wissler experimented with the use of such tests for predicting academic success.

Wissler (1901, p. 35) reported the following correlations between tests and average class standing (grade) for groups of students at Columbia:

	N	r
Reaction Time	227	—0.02
Marking A's	242	—0.09
Association	160	+0.08
Naming colors	112	+0.02
Logical memory	86	+0.19
Auditory memory	121	+0.16

He concluded that "the tests of quickness seem to hold a chance relation to class standing, and ability to do well in the memory tests has but little significance." Following

Wissler, there was little further effort to relate the tests then developed to academic performance.

Alfred Binet's development of the intelligence test opened new vistas for the testing movement. Since the individual intelligence tests were time-consuming and costly, they were not widely used for screening college applicants. The development of large-scale testing techniques during and following World War I, however, led to widespread use of intelligence or academic aptitude test scores for that purpose.

Using one of the newly-developed tests, Anderson (1920) reported a correlation of +.38 between first-semester grades and Army Alpha scores for 373 Yale freshmen. At about the same time, Jordan (1920) found a correlation of +.49 between Army Alpha scores and freshman grades for 485 students at the University of Arkansas.

The promising findings from studies of the correlation between college marks and the Army Alpha, the Stanford-Binet, and the Otis test generated great interest in the potentialities of aptitude or intelligence tests as college selection and placement devices. In the 1920's, four well-known college aptitude tests were developed: the CAVD by Thorndike, the American Council on Education Psychological Examination by Thurstone, the College Entrance Examination Board Scholastic Aptitude Test by Bingham, and the Ohio State Psychological Examination by Toops. Although there were many differences among these tests, they were alike in that they were designed specifically to measure academic aptitudes and, with the exception of the CAVD, they were developed for use exclusively at the college entrance or high school graduation level. All four of these tests in revised form are still in use, although the ACE Psychological Examination has been superseded by the School and College Ability Test.

In the 1920's, a large number of studies were reported on the relationship between scores on these tests and college performance. Segel (1934), in his review of college prediction studies, cited 103 reported correlations between general mental tests and college scholarship. Of the 103, eighty-three were in the range +.35 to +.54; nine were smaller than +.35; and only eleven of the 103 were greater than +.54.

At the time of Segel's report, psychologists and educators were generally convinced that much improved if not perfect prediction would soon be possible, contingent upon the further refinement of tests and prediction techniques. In 1946, nevertheless, Crawford and Burnham (1946) in their book, *Forecasting College Achievement,* reported that typical correlations between school and college averages and tests of general intelligence run between +.40 and +.50. Chauncey and Fredericksen (1951, pp. 90-92) pointed out that although correlations between various aptitude tests and freshmen grades may vary from zero to +.70, the median correlation would fall somewhere near +.45. They cited correlations between the C.E.E.B. Scholastic Aptitude Test and freshmen grades for several groups of Harvard freshmen. The correlations with verbal scores ranged from +.34 to +.52 with a median of +.44, while the correlations with mathematical scores ranged from +.25 to +.55 with a median value of +.47. Correlations between averaged C.E.E.B. achievement tests scores and freshman grades for the same groups ranged from +.54 to +.60. Similar findings were cited in a study of liberal arts freshmen at Princeton. In the *1957 Supplement*

to College Board Scores No. 2 (Fishman, 1957, pp. 7-8)
correlations between SAT verbal and mathematical scores
and first-term college grades were reported for student groups
in fourteen colleges. The thirty-eight correlations ranged from
+.14 to +.57, with a median value of +.35. In another
table in this publication, correlations between these test scores
and first-year college grades for fifteen groups in eleven colleges ranged from +.27 to +.59, with a median value
of +.41.

We could cite numerous other data. In any case, the point
seems clear that aptitude tests of various kinds have proved
to have some merit for the problem of predicting college
success. However, almost forty years of efforts to refine and
improve academic aptitude measures have not markedly
enhanced their effectiveness. Current findings of correlations
between such tests and college grades are almost identical
in level and precision to the correlations found in the 1920's,
a level of prediction which still leaves much room for
improvement.

Academic Predictors—
Achievement Test Scores

Though less widely used than school grades or aptitude
tests, achievement tests have been extensively tried in predictions of college success. The achievement test differs from
the aptitude test in that it is specifically designed to test
mastery of a special subject matter. At the same time that

intelligence and college aptitude tests were being developed, standardized tests of achievement in the high school subjects were becoming popular.

The Iowa Placement Examinations and the Iowa High School Content Examinations, initiated under the direction of Carl Seashore, represent one of the early major efforts to develop achievement tests which would be generally useful for college selection. These tests were designed to measure achievement and potential in common high school and college courses, e.g., English, mathematics, etc. In 1930, the Cooperative Test Service was established and soon a large number of Cooperative Achievement Tests were published. These were designed and used both for the selection of freshmen students and for measuring the achievement of college students through the sophomore year.

Achievement tests have proved to be equal or superior to aptitude tests for prediction of college success. In summarizing his analyses of prediction studies, Segel (1934, p. 70) concluded "that general achievement tests at the end of the high school course are more prognostic of general college scholarship than general mental tests." Segel's conclusion rested on the fact that the median of the correlation coefficients reported between general achievement tests and general college scholarship was significantly higher than the median of reported correlations between aptitude tests and college scholarship. He cited ten studies reporting correlations between achievement tests and college grades. The fourteen correlations reported had a median value of +.54; four of the eighteen exceeded +.64, and four were +.46 or below. Travers (1949, p. 155), too, reported that subject matter tests are generally second only to high school grades in their usefulness for prediction of college achievement.

Whatever the respective merits of aptitude versus achievement tests, the obvious point is that achievement tests are useful academic predictors. However, though they might be somewhat superior to aptitude tests, it seems clear that the general level and precision of predictions from achievement tests scores still leaves much to be desired. The College Board (Fishman, 1957, pp. 10-11) recently reported a number of studies of the correlations between C.E.E.B. Achievement Test scores and end-of-term grades in specific college courses, e.g., English Composition Test scores and freshmen English grades. The sixty-three correlations listed range from +.28 to +.75, with a median value of +.44.

Use of Academic Predictors in Combination

In addition to efforts to find a single predictor or type of data which will provide reliable estimates of academic success, many colleges combine several predictors in making such estimates. The most common procedure involves combining school grades and aptitude tests by using multiple correlation or regression techniques. The problem in such an approach is to find predictors that are relatively independent of one another. If grades and test scores were perfectly correlated, the use of both would not provide any better prediction than using either one separately. Since school grades and test scores are not perfectly correlated, they can be used together, and the combination will ordinarily provide somewhat improved estimates of probable college success. While school grades, aptitude test scores, or achievement test scores will ordinarily each correlate with college grades within the range +.40 to +.60, mutiple correlations using two or more of these in combination will usually be in the range +.55 to +.65.

Segel (1934), for example, cited sixteen studies in which high school marks had been combined with test scores or other indices to predict general college scholarship. Most of the correlations cited ranged from +.55 to +.65, with four writers reporting correlations over +.70. A number of studies reporting the results of combining variables were reviewed by Harris (1940). Nine studies reported correlations ranging from +.63 to +.71, when special combinations of academic predictors were used. In 1957, the College Board (Fishman, 1957, p. 8) reported fifteen correlations between first-year grades in college and combined predictors. The fifteen correlations ranged from +.52 to +.66, with a median value of +.61.

Other Approaches
to the Prediction Problem

The failure to find ways of significantly improving over-all predictions of college success is in part at least a result of the limitations of this formulation of the problem. Clearly, in addition to variations in grading standards, there are real differences in the demands of different courses and curricula. Such differences make the use of over-all criteria, such as average grade, inadequate. Moreover, there is much evidence to show that college success is in part a function of qualities or attributes not directly related to intellectual ability. Such qualities as motivation, interest, study habits, personality, and social adjustment are just a few of the factors that have been shown to affect academic success or have been suggested as relevant variables.

Attempts to take account of the above limitations have been in two directions. First, there have been a large number of efforts to include or exclude other variables. For example, in using average grades to determine success, marks in such courses as physical education or military training are often excluded. Alternatively, there have been a large number of efforts to include measures of interest, adjustment, or motivation in the prediction studies. With few exceptions, such attempts have led to little improvement in the effectiveness of predictions.

A second approach consists of a reformulation of the problem. Two major approaches have been tried, differential prediction and assessment techniques. Of these, differential prediction has received more attention and use. Unlike the studies in which one or more measures are combined in order to arrive at the best estimate of an average mark, differential prediction usually involves obtaining measures of different traits or achievements. Estimates are then made of subject areas in which the student is likely to be most successful and subject areas in which he will probably be only moderately successful or unsuccessful.

Crawford and Burnham (1946, pp. 136-137), for example, outline a sample aptitude battery composed of the following tests:

I. SAT—Verbal facility (The College Board Scholastic Aptitude Test, Verbal Section, taken prior to matriculation).

II. ALT—Linguistic aptitude, as measured by an Artificial Language Test.

III. VRT—Verbal Reasoning Test (logical inference, deductive judgment, etc.).

IV. QRT—Quantitative Reasoning Test (ability in manipulating hypothetical quantitative data so as to perceive relations or principles characterizing them and derive laws analogous to, yet different from, those actually encountered in study of the natural sciences).

V. MAT—Mathematical aptitude (the present mathematical section of the Scholastic Aptitude Test).

VI. SVT—Spatial Visualizing Test (representation of three-dimensional forms by two-dimensional figures through projections, block-counting, etc.).

VII. MIT—Mechanical Ingenuity Test (problems in gear or pulley movements, structural ability and mechanical operations).

Crawford and Burnham argued that by analyzing a student's scores on such a battery one could identify variations within the student group as a whole and differences in relative capacity within the same individual. From such an analysis a student could be shown to be more promising for some subject areas than for others. They suggested, for example, that scores I, II, and III are especially significant for prognosis in liberal arts study; III, IV, V for pure science and mathematics; and V, VI, and VII for applied sciences such as engineering.

Extensive data reported by Crawford and Burnham showed significant differences between correlations of test scores and freshman marks in various subjects. For example, the SAT verbal score (I) correlated with average English and history grades +.49, with physics grades +.40, with average mathematics and drawing grades +.16, and with engineering drawing grades +.11 (1944 Yale freshman). Correlations between different test scores and grades in courses ranged from +.57 to −.01, for two freshman populations. When *achievement tests* are used instead of grades, the correlations with aptitude tests tend to be higher although the pattern of differences remains substantially the same. More recently, Horst (1957) did extensive research on differential predictions at the University of Washington. On cross validation, he found the correlations with the predicted criteria range from +.13 to +.71.

Much research, using factor analysis and other complex statistical techniques, has been done on differential measurement and prediction. Thurstone's (1938) work, *Primary Mental Abilities,* for example, is one of the most systematic efforts to apply factor analysis to the separation and measurement of different abilities. Efforts to relate this battery and

many others, e.g., the Iowa Aptitude tests and various sets
of the Cooperative tests, have shown that differential predictions of the level and magnitude of the Crawford and
Burnham findings can be replicated, but they have rarely
been exceeded. Correlations between grades, however categor-
ized, and test scores, however organized, still tend to fall in
the $+.40$ to $+.60$ range, with only occasional correlations
reaching $+.70$.

Assessment Approaches to Prediction

Another approach to the prediction problem uses the assessment techniques. Its proponents have suggested that the
usual formulation of the problem is essentially static and consequently does not take into account the interplay between
changing individual needs and capacities and changing social
and situational demands. The latter affect the behavior of the
individual as well as the ways in which his behavior will be
judged (graded).

They have proposed, alternatively, that better predictions
could be made if the investigators would study the situation
in which the student will be operating and from this derive
a model personality which hypothetically describes the kind
of person most likely to fulfill the demands of the situation.
Predictions of academic success have been derived from a
comparison of the student with this model. H. A. Murray,
in his introduction to the volume, *Methods in Personality*

Assessment, (Stern, Stein, Bloom, 1956, pp. 19-20) illustrated the differences in approach in the following paragraph:

   A little caricature might serve to sharpen our awareness of
the step that has been taken by Professors Stern, Stein, and
Bloom. Let us assume that the assignment is to predict grades
in an English course given by Professor X. Responding to this
challenge, psychologists of the old school would devote almost
all their time to the construction of tests, let us say, of verbal
facility, literary appreciation, and so forth, and combine these
with a test of general intelligence to provide a measure of "aptitude for English studies." The authors of this volume, on the
other hand, would start by obtaining as much information as
possible about Professor X's tastes, especially the explicit and
implicit standards that determine his grading of term papers
and of final examinations. They would ask the Professor what
special merits he saw in his best students and what particular
objections he had to those he esteemed least. They would also con-
duct a systematic examination of the students who had received
the highest grades in Professor X's course. This model would
constitute a target. Then, having clearly defined it, and not before, these psychologists would apply themselves to the task of
selecting and devising instruments to measure the extent to
which each applicant's personality approximates the model. In
short, they would formulate—much more specifically than have
previous assessors—the demands of the prospective situation,
the kinds of persons who have met those demands successfully,
and the system of values of the judge or judges who will make
the ratings with which the assessment scores will eventually
be compared.

Several methodological approaches to the assessment technique have been developed by Stern, Stein, and Bloom, in-
cluding some less time-consuming than Murray's caricature
implied. A number of studies of the efficiency of the new
methods have been made with very promising results. As yet,

however, large-scale applications of the assessment techniques for selection or admission of students have not been
developed.

Academic Prediction
at Different Levels of Education

In the foregoing summary of studies and reports on academic prediction we have looked only at the problem of predicting first-year undergraduate college grades from data
secured at the high school level. It should be noted, however,
that the problem of academic choice or selection at this level
has parallels at other educational levels. As indicated before,
in England the principal focus of interest is on the transition
from primary schools to secondary schools, and McClelland
(1942), and Yates and Pidgeon (1957) studied the problem
at this level.

The transition from undergraduate college to graduate or
professional schools has received much attention in this country. Dewey Stuit (1949) has summarized the studies of
prediction of performance in graduate school in his volume,
Predicting Success in Professional Schools. It is interesting
to note that the present efficiency of prediction at the professional school level is about the same as at the college level.
Thus Stuit remarked that the magnitude of correlation coefficients that appear in the literature and are used in
prediction are usually between $+.25$ and $+.70$, with the vast
majority between $+.30$ and $+.60$. Clearly there is as much

room for improvement here as at the college level. Although our research was restricted to the latter, there is no reason to believe that techniques of adjusting grades may not be just as effective for predictions at the professional and graduate school level.

Purpose of This Study

From our review of the literature on prediction, it is clear that three different types of evidence have been found to be useful in making predictions of college grades. Each of the three—high school grades, aptitude test scores, and achievement test scores—has been widely used both singly and in various combinations. But the levels of prediction efficiency, as reflected in correlation coefficients, have remained practically unchanged. This study represents another attempt to make more accurate predictions.

The design of the study, however, represents a somewhat different approach from most prior studies. Rather than search for a new variable or index or some method of combining indices, we began by asking if we might find more effective ways of interpreting available data, especially high school and college grades. In so doing, we were only borrowing a method that has long been used by school counselors and college admissions officers. That is, such persons as a matter of course do place different values on grades from different institutions, and though such procedures might lead to some error, few people would doubt that similar grades from different institutions often represent different levels of attainment. Our study was a search for ways of more efficiently accounting for such differences among institutions.

We had a hunch that one might use aptitude test scores or experience records to adjust grades from different schools. For example, it seemed possible that if one student came from a class whose average aptitude was high and another student came from a class whose average aptitude was relatively lower and both students had the same grade average the first would be a better college risk than the latter. Later we found that a number of other investigators had had the same hunch and that in fact the general method had proved effective in other studies. Our case must rest, however, with the findings of our own analysis. In the next chapter we have described several methods of adjusting grades and the effects of such adjustments on academic prediction. In the following chapters we have tried to indicate some of the implications of these findings and some of the potential consequences of the application of Academic Predictor Scales. We know that these techniques are no more than techniques; they will not solve the critical problems of college choice and college selection. Adjusted grades can be used wisely or unwisely; and, because of institutional sensitivity, they may not be used at all. Yet we submit that in our present state of knowledge, scaled grades can be used to greatly reduce gross errors in choice and selection, and in this way much of the waste and frustration of our present high rate of college failure can be reduced.

National Registration Office Data

Before we proceed to describe the methods and findings of the study, a word needs to be said about the data. For a number of years the University Examiner's Office at the University of Chicago has prepared the annual reports of the National Registration Office. As a consequence, we had available the records of some 25,000 students who had graduated from the 126 participating schools and who had subsequently gone on to college. We had a complete record of all of these students' high school achievement and college transcripts covering their first year of college work. For about 5,000 of these students we had College Board test scores. All of our samples were taken from the N.R.O. population.

Although a few public high schools are members of N.R.O., most of the schools are independent, privately supported schools. While analysis of grade distributions and distributions of group aptitude levels reveals that a wide range of school populations is represented in the sample, it cannot be assumed that our sample is an adequate sample of all secondary schools. There is no reason to believe, however, that the problem is unique to private schools, or that the two types of schools are so different that the procedures would be less effective if applied to a broader range of schools.

In 1952, with the support of the National Registration Office, we undertook a small exploratory study of the possibilities of scaling grades. The results were promising and in

1956 the National Registration Office for Independent Schools and the National Council of Independent Schools gave the University Examiner's Office a grant for further research. This grant was used to support the studies reported here.

2

The Effectiveness of Different
Scaling Methods

Some Standards for Comparison

BEFORE DESCRIBING VARI-
ous techniques for scaling secondary school and college
grades it is well to set some bench marks to indicate, rather
generally, the limits within which we might expect correlations between secondary school and college grades.

A very obvious lower limit to these correlations is the relationship between secondary school and college freshman
grades when no correction method is applied. For three samples of students in the N.R.O. populations, we found correlations * of +.51 (N=1226), +.51 (N=5723) and +.49

---

* All correlations reported here are product moment correlations unless
otherwise specified.

(N=2238) between school and college freshman grades. Crawford and Burnham (1946, p. 89), summarizing the literature on academic prediction, reported +.50 as an average correlation between school and college grades. It seems reasonable to use +.50 as a good approximation of the level of correlation between high school grades and college freshman grades when they have not been scaled or adjusted. As has been shown in Chapter 1, this has been a relatively stable value for approximately forty or more years. This lower limit must be significantly exceeded if scaling procedures are to be regarded as effective.

Setting a theoretical upper limit to the correlation is a bit more difficult. Why not expect a perfect correlation between school and college grades? Although we do not have a good index of the reliability of average grades, we know that the correlation between grades of different instructors is far from perfect. We also expect that the student will change from year to year so that at no time can we predict with perfect certainty what he will do in the future.

Since our major concern in scaling grades is to take into consideration institutional variation, we may derive some notion of the upper limit or the level of attainable prediction from data where institutional variation is eliminated. Obviously this would be true of correlations between grade averages *within* schools or colleges. Frederiksen and Schrader (1951) reported fourteen correlations between college grade averages for different semesters for non-veteran students. The median correlations between grade averages for adjacent semesters (e.g., first semester vs. second semester, second vs. third semester, and third vs. fourth semester) was +.79. The median correlation between grade averages two semesters apart (e.g., first vs. third semester, and second vs. fourth semester) was $+.72$, while the median correlation between grade averages three semesters apart (e.g., first vs. fourth semester) was $+.66$.

It is likely that these correlations reflect some combination of the unreliability of grades and real changes taking place in the student. As time increases, such changes are more likely to occur and will consequently reduce the possibility of prediction. Unpublished studies made at the University of Chicago, where grades are based on carefully constructed comprehensive examinations, show correlations of $+.87$ between first- and second-year college grades. This would suggest that even with highly objective and reliable grading procedures the upper level we might possibly seek to attain in correlations of scaled high school grade averages and scaled college freshman grade averages is of the order of $+.80$ to $+.87$ if we could eliminate the effect of institutional variation in standards.

A more realistic approach to the determination of possible upper limits is to study the actual relationships between the grades of particular school-college combinations. A particular high school may send several of its students to College A, some to College B, and some to College C. Although the number of students involved in each of these school-college combinations may be relatively small, it is instructive to study these combinations.

An example is afforded by an eastern school that, in 1956, sent sixty-eight of its students to thirty-four colleges. Twenty-eight of these students went to seven colleges. In Table 2 the high school grades of these twenty-eight students are shown in relation to the freshman grades they made in these seven colleges. One obvious fact shown in this table is that different segments of the high school group went to different colleges. Thus, the students who went to College B all had high school grade averages of 3.4 or better, while the students who went to College A had high school grade averages of 2.4 or better. Those who went to College F had high school grade averages of 2.3 or less, and those who went to College G had high school grade averages of 2.1 or less. Thus, the more able students (scholastically) from this high school went to some colleges while the less able attended other colleges. What caused this sorting out—counseling, selection, and/or voluntary choice —cannot be determined with the data available. However, it is this type of evidence that makes clear the likelihood of gross differences in the scholastic achievement of students in different colleges.

The striking point is that in spite of the gross differences in the previous academic achievement of the students, the distributions of absolute grades assigned in the different colleges are very similar. Thus, the average college grade of the six students in College A is approximately 2.8 (B—) while the average grades of the four students in College F is 2.9 (B—). Similar comparisons could be made with the other colleges in Table 2. This evidence suggests that college grading standards are different and that grades are sensitive primarily to the variation of students *within* the college.

Table 2—Grade Averages in Selected Colleges Shown in Relation to Grades Made in High School X for Twenty-eight Students

GRADE AVERAGE IN HIGH SCHOOL X	GRADE AVERAGES IN COLLEGE						
	College A	College B	College C	College D	College E	College F	College G
3.7	3.1						
3.6							
		3.6					
3.5		3.1		3.1			
		3.0					
3.4	3.3	2.3					
3.3							
3.2	3.0						
3.1	2.4		2.5				
3.0			2.9				
			2.8				
2.9							
2.8							
2.7					2.7		
2.6	2.3		2.3				
2.5				2.2			
2.4	2.5						
2.3					2.3	3.2	
2.2				2.1	1.3		
2.1							2.8
2.0						3.0	2.0
							2.7
1.9							2.5
1.8						2.8	
1.7							
1.6							
1.5							
1.4						2.8	
1.3							
1.2							

It is, however, a somewhat different phenomenon in Table 2 that is relevant to the present consideration of limits. As we glance down each column of the table, it becomes evident that the college grades of the students are roughly in the same order as their high school grades. With two exceptions, the six students in College A rank in college in the same order they did in high school. All the students in Colleges B, D, E, and F are in the same rank order in college and high school. There is one exception in College C and College G. Thus, if we study the cases college by college, there would be only four, out of a total of twenty-eight, students out of order in these school-college combinations.

If we took these twenty-eight cases and classified them as high or low on college grades, irrespective of the college attended, and high or low on grades made in High School X, we would find the following relationship:

Table 3—Comparison of Grades Made in High Schools and Colleges

	Low in college grades (2.7-)	High in college grades (2.8+)
High in high school grades (2.7+)	4	9
Low in high school grades (2.6-)	10	5
		Total = 28

Using our crude classifications, nineteen out of twenty-eight, or 68 per cent of the cases, receive the same classification in high school and college.

A completely different picture results if we classify the students within each of the high school–college sub-groups. Thus for the combination of high school–college A, we may divide the six students into the high and low in College A

(3.0+ or better and less than 3.0). We may also divide these students into those who were (among only these six students) relatively high and low in high school (3.2+ or better and 3.1 or less). This may be done within each of the high school–college sub-groups in Table 2. In effect, we are now asking whether each sub-group of students maintains roughly the same classification within the college as they did in high school. A table corresponding to Table 3 is the following:

Table 4—Comparison of Relative Grades Made in High Schools and Colleges

	Relatively low in college grades	Relatively high in college grades
Relatively high in high school grades	1	14
Relatively low in high school grades	11	2
		Total = 28

Using these crude relative classifications, twenty-five out of twenty-eight or 89 per cent of the cases receive the same relative classification in high school and college.

We applied this same type of relative classification to 500 cases selected from our larger set of data. These 500 cases divided into sixty-nine high school–college sub-groups with three or more students in each sub-group (the average sub-group had seven students). For these 500 cases, the relative classifications resulted in the following table:

Table 5—Comparison of Relative Grades Made in High Schools and Colleges

	Relatively low in college grades	Relatively high in college grades
Relatively high in high school grades	40	203
Relatively low in high school grades	214	43
		Total = 500

We found that out of these 500 cases, 417 or 83 per cent of the students maintained their same relative position in high school and college.

This, however, is a very crude way of analyzing the data. The rank order correlation method is appropriate for finding the extent to which students maintain their same relative rank order on two variables. We found 154 sub-groups in our data where seven or more students were involved in each high school–college combination. These sub-groups had an average size of twelve and there were 1,869 students in all. Using the method of rank correlation we found that the median rank correlation for these 154 sub-groups was +.65. This figure is higher than the average correlation of +.50 found by different investigators between high school and college grades when grades are taken at their absolute value (an A is regarded as equivalent at each school or college and likewise for the B, C, etc.).

Table 6—Rank Correlations Between High School and College Grades for High School-College Sub-groups

Rank Correlation	Number of Sub-groups	Per Cent
90-99	8	5
80-89	25	16
70-79	28	18
60-69	31	20
50-59	23	15
40-49	16	11
30-39	11	7
20-29	2	1
10-19	4	3
0-9	2	1
Less than 0	4	3
Total Number of Sub-groups	154	100

This +.65 could be taken as an approximation of the upper limit of relationship between high school and college grades if it were not evident that each sub-group represents a relatively homogeneous group (at least on the basis of high school grades). The effect of such homogeneity is to lower the correlations.

The distribution of rank correlations for these 154 sub-groups is shown in Table 6. It will be noted that 5 per cent of the sub-groups have rank correlations of +.90 or higher, while 21 per cent have rank correlations of +.80 or higher. We are of the opinion that the +.80 represents a realistic upper limit since about a fifth of the sub-groups reach this level or higher. Table 6 is also informative in showing that about one-fourth of the sub-groups has rank correlations of less than +.50, while 39 per cent have rank correlations of

+.70 or higher. This suggests that there is considerable variation in the predictive value of grades in different high school–college sub-groups. This makes it clear that any method of adjusting grades is likely to produce somewhat different results in the various schools and colleges.

In the following sections we will report on the effect of several different methods of scaling or correcting grades. The results achieved by each of these methods may be compared with the limits of +.50 to +.80 suggested here. Ideally the method should attain the maximum value and still be practicable for use in high schools and colleges. The methods will be referred to as the Internal Method, the Aptitude Method, and the Achievement Method.

The Internal Method

Almost every admissions officer in a college or university has some way of taking into consideration the variation in standards among secondary schools. He remembers the sad experiences the faculty has had with students from some schools and the excellent records made by students from other schools. The admissions officer may have a few notes in his files about particular schools or he may keep much of this in his memory. While he may be very adept in the use of this stored information, he has difficulty in passing it on to his successors. Unfortunately, even memory is deceptive and places more emphasis on exceptional and dramatic incidents than on less vivid events or instances. A somewhat more systematic record of experience is needed.

As was pointed out in Chapter 1, some colleges and universities attempt to develop systematic experience tables in which they compile the grades received in their college by students from different secondary schools (Chauncey and Frederiksen, 1951, pp. 90-92). They refer to these data when considering new applicants from a listed school. Undoubtedly similar experience tables are developed by some guidance persons in the secondary schools.

These experience tables, which relate the grades earned in schools to the grades received by the same students in colleges, are illustrative of the Internal Method we have used in this study. The simplest example of the Internal Method would be found if a secondary school sent all of its graduates to one college. (There are probably some secondary school– junior college combinations that approximate this example.) Although the college may grade more severely than the secondary school, the exact relation between the school grades and college grades could be determined. For example, we might find that students with a C average in the school receive a D average in the college, students with a B average in school receive a C average in the college, and students with an A average in school receive a B average in college. Such a simple adjustment becomes a bit more complicated when we have hundreds of secondary schools sending students to hundreds of colleges.

In our work we have attempted to find the best fit between high school and college grades by correcting high school grades on the basis of college grades and in turn correcting college grades on the basis of high school grades.* There are a variety of methods that might be employed to do this. Our method consisted of the following six steps.

Step 1

We divided all the colleges in our sample into three groups on the basis of the grading standards employed. In type I we put those colleges where the students received somewhat higher average grades than they had received in secondary school. In type II we put those colleges where the students received about the same average grades as they had received in secondary school. In type III we put those colleges where the students received lower average grades than they had received in secondary school.

Step 2

We then found the correlation between the secondary-school grades and college grades in each of the three types of colleges and by means of a regression equation determined the college grades that would be predicted from the high-school grades.† This regression of high school on college

---

* In these calculations high school grades refer to the average grade made by the student in high school, and college grades refer to the average grade made by the student in his freshman college year.

† See Statistical Appendix.

grades thus gave us a way of modifying the college grades in each type of college to take into consideration the difference in standards among the colleges. In effect what we did was to determine the average school grade required to make a specific grade in each type of college. In Table 7 we have shown how the original college grade averages were modified for each type of college. These modified values, which were based on about 18,000 student records, are as follows:

Table 7—Modified Values Assigned to College Grades in Each Type of College

ORIGINAL COLLEGE GRADE AVERAGES	MODIFIED GRADE AVERAGES FOR EACH TYPE OF COLLEGE		
	Type I	Type II	Type III
4 (A)	3.00	3.40	3.67
3 (B)	2.35	2.77	3.13
2 (C)	1.80	2.20	2.59
1 (D)	1.40	1.86	2.00
0 (F)	......	1.00	......

It will be noted that on a five-point scale (0—4), the student who receives a college average of 4 in a type III institution has made a modified college grade average of 3.67, while the student who receives a college average of 4 in a type I institution has received a modified college grade average of only 3.00.

Step 3

We then substituted the modified grade for the actual college grade average received by each student, depending on which one of the three types of colleges he had attended. In this and in the succeeding steps the sample consisted of 4,519 students who entered college in 1955 or 1956.

Step 4

The 4,519 students were then sorted into groups on the basis of the secondary schools from which they had come and the correlations between their secondary-school and modified college grade averages were determined for each school. The regression of modified college grade averages on school grade averages was determined for each school and these new values were substituted for the student's school grade averages. This is illustrated for three schools:

Table 8—Adjusted Values Assigned to School Grades in Three Selected Schools

ORIGINAL SCHOOL GRADE AVERAGES	ADJUSTED SCHOOL GRADE AVERAGES		
	School A	School B	School C
4 (A)	2.88	3.04	3.18
3 (B)	2.29	2.64	2.82
2 (C)	1.86	2.20	2.37
1 (D)	1.40	1.81	2.07
0 (F)	.98	1.45	1.57

It will be noted that for School C a grade of 2 is replaced by 2.37, while for School A it is replaced by 1.86. Thus School C students received higher adjusted school grades than School B students and, in turn, School B students received higher adjusted school grades than did School A students.

Step 5

The students were then sorted into groups on the basis of the specific colleges they had attended, and the correlations between the adjusted school grade averages and the actual college grade averages were determined for each college. The regression of the adjusted school grade averages on the college grade averages was determined for each college and these new values were used to adjust the students' college grade averages. This is illustrated for three colleges:

**Table 9—Adjusted Values Assigned to College Grades
    in Three Selected Colleges**

ORIGINAL COLLEGE GRADE AVERAGES	ADJUSTED GRADE AVERAGE		
	College X	College Y	College Z
4 (A)	2.66	2.99	3.20
3 (B)	2.36	2.70	2.88
2 (C)	2.06	2.41	2.56
1 (D)	1.76	2.12	2.24
0 (F)	1.46	1.83	1.82

It will be noted that for College Z a grade of 2 is replaced by 2.56 while for College X it is replaced by 2.06. Thus, the College Z adjusted value for a grade of C is higher than for College Y and in turn College Y is higher than College X.

Step 6

The correlation between the adjusted school grades (Step 4) and the adjusted college grades (Step 5) was determined. This correlation for the 4,519 students who entered college in 1955 or 1956 was $+.77$. Thus, by adjusting school and college grades for institutional variation we have increased the correlation between school and college grades from about $+.50$ to $+.77$. This is a substantial increase and indicates that an adjustment of grades for school and college variation in standards results in marked improvement in the efficiency of prediction.

However, we have here maximized the correlation by adjusting the school and college grades of a particular sample of students to each other. What happens if we then apply the same adjustments to a new population of students from the same schools and colleges? When we apply the corrections determined on the 1955 and 1956 group to 2,115 students who entered college in 1957 we find the correlation between adjusted school and college grade averages to be $+.72$. Thus, there is very little shrinkage in our correlation when a new group of students is used. This suggests that a correction based on one year's group of students can be applied to a succeeding group of students and still attain a high level of prediction. Whether marked shrinkage in the predictions will occur as the same corrections are applied in succeeding years is not known.

The Internal Method involves a minimum number of assumptions. It assumes that the grade earned at one level of education should be adjusted to the grade earned at another level of education. That is, that the appropriate criteria for high school grades are college grades and vice versa. It further assumes that linear quantitative methods are appropriate to such grade adjustments. It includes the assumption that the grade scale for a school or college can be derived from the summarization of school-college grades for a sample of the students from that school or college.

An additional assumption involved in this method is that the adjustment to grades made on the basis of one group of students will be appropriate to succeeding groups of students. While we have shown that this assumption is reasonable for at least one year, we would hesitate at this point to assume that the same adjustment would apply for many years. We would expect that in a period of rapid change in the proportion of high school graduates entering college as well as change in selection and admission procedures, considerable adjustment in the scale values for particular colleges and secondary schools might be needed regularly. We would recommend that if this method of adjusting grades is adopted, a careful check be maintained to determine how frequently the scale must be revised. In the early years of its use, it should be adjusted each year if possible, especially since its use may bring about marked shifts in the grading standards of some schools and colleges.

It is clear from the foregoing material that the method of internal adjustment yields a very high level of prediction of college grades. The value of $+.72$ is not too far from the upper limit of $+.80$ based on estimates described at the beginning of this chapter. If it were practicable this method would be the ideal method of treating grades.

The major difficulty in using the Internal Method is that it requires a central organization to process the data. The barriers to be overcome in order to put the Internal Method into actual operation on a national basis are exceedingly great. One of the problems would be the collection and processing of the data since this would require the annual collection and analysis of almost a million records from thousands of schools and colleges. The availability of high speed computing devices could make the processing and reporting of results very rapid and quite inexpensive. Probably the greatest barrier would be the resistance of many school and college people to the adjustment of their grading scales and to the release of these data to other schools and colleges.

Although the Internal Method would be most effective on a national basis, establishment on a state basis is more likely of immediate realization. Although this would make it inapplicable to students who go to out-of-state colleges, Hungate (1957) estimated that *80* per cent of students in higher educational institutions are residents of the state in which the college or university is located. This leads us to believe that the Internal Method could be applied to the high schools and colleges within a state with considerable effectiveness. If the states adopting these procedures are able to markedly reduce college failures and drop-outs within a few years, it is possible that such results would enable a national grading scale to be developed within a relatively brief period of time.

Still another alternative for the implementation of the Internal Method is the further development of the National Registration Office or some similar agency to process the school and college grades for secondary schools and colleges willing to subscribe to such a service. The improved prediction, appropriate placement of students, and reduced failure rate in college should soon more than justify the time and money expended for the service. Perhaps the relative magnitude of costs can be appreciated best if one considers that the costs of the service for all the students in the largest secondary school need be only a fraction of the amount spent by one failing student (or his parents) for one year of college. It should be remembered that the scale values for any secondary school or college would be based only on those students who had actually entered college and completed the first year of work.

The Aptitude Method

The Internal Method requires that the scale values be determined by some organization that secures both school and college grades for a sizeable number of students. While the organization may function at a state or national level or as an independent organization for a group of secondary schools, and colleges, it requires a great deal of organizational talent to get it started. An alternative possibility is to develop correction methods that would enable a particular school or college to determine its own scale values and to communicate these values to other schools or colleges as it desires. If this could be done, it would simplify procedures greatly, and would enable scale values to be developed and used as rapidly as individual schools or colleges are ready.

The requirement for a scale that can be used by individual schools or colleges is to have another criterion or scale which is available to the school or college. Such a criterion must have a relatively high relationship with grades and must be available for individual students. In 1933, Toops (1933) suggested the use of an aptitude test for this purpose.

Our second method entails the use of a scholastic aptitude test as the external criterion for adjusting school and college grades. We shall refer to this as the Aptitude Method. In his research, Peters (1952) made use of a scholastic aptitude test to correct grades. He found this improved the relationship between school and college grades from a correlation of +.53 to +.67. As cited in Chapter 1, Rietz (1934), McClelland (1942), and Yates and Pidgeon (1957) have also reported the use of aptitude test scores for adjusting grades.

The aptitude levels of students vary considerably from educational institution to educational institution. In order to show something of the variation at the college level, we selected some of the results reported for the American Council on Education Psychological Examination in 1937. The manual (Thurstone and Thurstone, 1938) for the 1937 tests reports results from 323 colleges that had tested their entering students. In the college with the highest group of students, the mean score was equivalent to the 90th percentile, while in the college with the lowest group, the mean score was equivalent to the 8th percentile. Another way of interpreting this difference is to note that on the basis of the quartile deviations one would not expect students in the highest college to have scores which overlapped with students in the lowest college. In order to illustrate the variation from col-

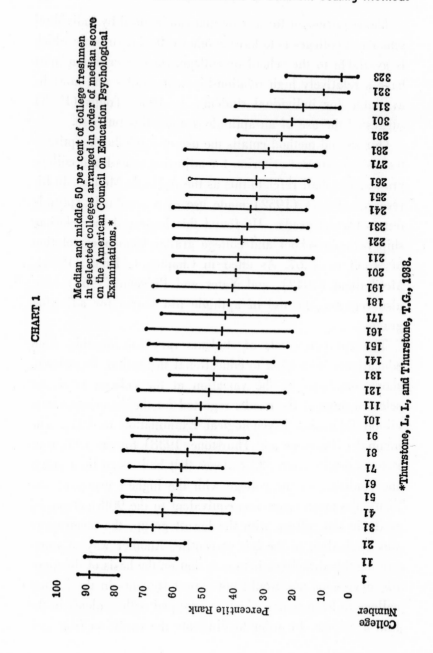

CHART 1

Median and middle 50 per cent of college freshmen in selected colleges arranged in order of median score on the American Council on Education Psychological Examinations.*

*Thurstone, L. L., and Thurstone, T.G., 1938.

lege to college more graphically, we have selected every 10th college and plotted its mean and quartile deviation (the middle 50 per cent of students) in Chart 1.

The College Entrance Examination Board (Fishman, 1957, pp. 23-27) reports almost equally great difference for the Verbal Score on the Scholastic Aptitude Test. In this report results are presented for 150 student groups in liberal arts colleges. The highest liberal arts college student group had a mean of 672 (95th percentile), while the lowest college group had a mean of 406 (19th percentile). In another comparison of College Board Scores on page 31 of the same reference, all of the students in one college have Verbal Scores on the Scholastic Aptitude Test higher than the average student score in the lowest college.

When we turn to the secondary school level, we find much the same variation from school to school. The 1952 edition of the ACE Psychological Examination was administered to senior students in 134 independent high schools. Data were reported by the Educational Records Bureau (1953). Here the highest school had a median of 152.5 (97th percentile), while the lowest school had a median of 77.5 (16th percentile). In order to emphasize the variation from school to school, we have selected every seventh school and plotted the median percentile rank of its students in Chart 2.

Scholastic Aptitude Test scores were available for almost 3,000 students in the N.R.O. population. Here we find much the same results as reported in the foregoing. At the secondary level, the highest school had a verbal mean score of 632 (90th percentile) while the lowest school had a mean score of 426 (24th percentile). At the college level, using only

CHART 2

Median of high school seniors in selected independent
secondary schools arranged in order of median score
on the American Council on Education Psychological
Examination*

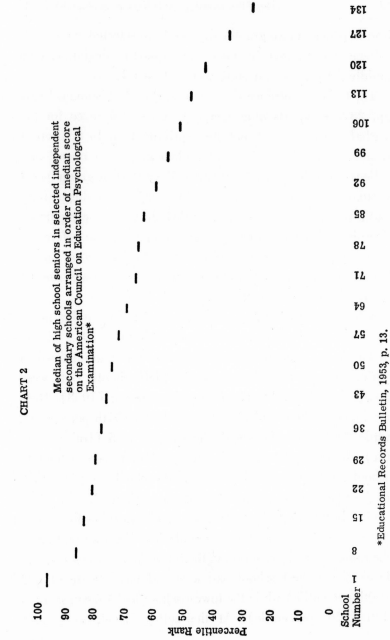

*Educational Records Bulletin, 1953, p. 13.

colleges for which there were 15 or more students in the 1956 group, we find a high verbal mean score of 654 (93rd percentile) and a low mean score of 428 (24th percentile).

Thus, using different aptitude tests, different years, and different groups of schools and colleges, we find tremendous variation in the scholastic aptitude of students enrolled in different schools and colleges. It is likely that this variation in scholastic aptitude would be reflected in some way in the grading standards used. Thus in Chart 1, if we assume that the average student in the highest college is given a C grade and that the average student in the lowest college is also given a C grade, it seems unlikely that these two C grades represent the same levels of academic attainment.

The basic assumption underlying the Aptitude Method is that students with high levels of intelligence or scholastic aptitude achieve at a higher academic level than do students with lower levels of intelligence or scholastic aptitude. This assumption rests in part on the fact that within a school or college it is likely that aptitude scores and academic grades correlate approximately $+.50$. It also rests on the observation that teachers set their instruction to the level of ability of the students in their classes. Thus, although the teachers may distribute the usual range of grades to the students, the level of instruction and learning is likely to be responsive to the level of ability of the students.

Although there may be some question about the reasoning behind the Aptitude Method, the central issue is whether or not this method of adjusting school and college grades yields and college grades. The effectiveness of this method may be better predictions than those based on the uncorrected school judged by comparing resulting correlations with those obtained using the Internal Method or uncorrected grades.

We have employed two statistical procedures in estimating the adjusted grades by the Aptitude Method. In one technique we have determined the mean aptitude score made by the students receiving each grade average in a particular school. Thus in one school if ten students receive grade averages of A and they average 700 on a scholastic aptitude test (where the mean score for the national group is 500 and the standard deviation is 100), the grade of A in that school is designated at 700. If fourteen students in that school receive a grade average of B and they average 630 on the scholastic aptitude test, the grade of B is designated as 630. This is the process by which each grade level in each school and college is converted into a scaled score. The mean technique is thus a method by which the mean aptitude score for each sub-group of students is substituted for the letter or numerical grade received by that sub-group. This technique is most dependable where sizeable numbers of students are available at each grade level since a mean aptitude score based on two or three cases will count just as much as a mean based on thirty or more cases.

We were able to find 1,827 students in the 1956 N.R.O. population for whom we had scores on the Scholastic Aptitude Test of the College Entrance Examination Board. Using this sample of students we applied the Aptitude Method (mean) to both secondary school and college grades. We used the combined verbal and mathematical score as the criterion for adjusting grades.

The Aptitude Method (mean) applied to grades at both

the secondary school and college level yielded a correlation of +.72 between adjusted high school grade averages and adjusted college freshman grade averages. Strikingly enough, this is the same correlation as the one obtained for the 1957 group by the Internal Method. This Aptitude Method appears to be a useful scaling method as compared with the uncorrected grade correlation of +.50.

Another statistical technique we tried with the Aptitude Method is the regression technique. In this technique, the correlation between scholastic aptitude and grades in each school or college was determined. Using the mean and standard deviation of grades and scholastic aptitude scores, the scholastic aptitude value of each grade was determined by computing the regression of scholastic aptitude scores on grades. This technique makes each value dependent on the entire group of students and is not as subject to errors arising from a small number of cases at a particular grade level as is the mean technique. It does, however, involve the assumption that the relation between grades and scholastic aptitude is linear; that is, for each increment in scholastic aptitude it is assumed that there is an increment in grades. The effect of the regression technique is to bring the scaled grades closer to the over-all scale mean of the school or college than is the case with the mean technique. This technique of correcting school and college grades when applied to 2,959 students in the N.R.O. population for the years 1956 and 1957 yielded a correlation of +.75. The regression technique thus yielded a slightly higher correlation than the mean technique.

It is of interest to note that when we attempted to do a

type of cross-validation by applying the Aptitude Method corrections to the results for different years, the regression technique was more stable than the mean technique. Thus, applying the 1956-1957 corrections to data for 1,200 college entrants in 1951 yielded correlations of $+.61$ for the mean technique and $+.66$ for the regression technique. In view of the time span of five years, this was a very severe test of the Aptitude Method since it involved both the possibility of actual change in aptitude scores of the students in the different schools and colleges as well as changes in the grading standards. It would be a more appropriate test if the scale could be recomputed, using the aptitude scores for the 1951 group. Unfortunately, we did not have the aptitude data necessary for this computation. We did however break the 1956 and 1957 college entrants into two groups and found that the Aptitude Method (regression) yielded correlations of $+.72$ for 1956 (N=1412) and $+.77$ (N=1547) for 1957. Further types of cross-validation are needed. However, the data here presented do suggest that the Aptitude Method is a relatively stable correction, especially if regression procedures are used.

Yates and Pidgeon (1957) used the aptitude scores to relate elementary school teachers' estimates to secondary school grades. They used a somewhat simpler technique than we have employed here. In each school, they ranked the students by teachers' estimates. They also listed in order the aptitude scores made by the students in that school. Then, they substituted the aptitude score for the teachers' estimate of the same rank order. Thus the student who had the highest achievement value in a particular school was given the highest aptitude score for that school. The student who had the next highest achievement value was assigned the second highest aptitude score, and so on. The effect of this technique was to give the average student in the school the average aptitude score of that school and to relate the variation in the achievement estimates to the variation in the aptitude scores. Yates and Pidgeon (1957) regarded this as a relatively rough procedure which is justified by the simplicity of the clerical procedures required. They reported correlations of $+.82$ between elementary and secondary school teachers' estimates corrected by this method. We studied a sample of 67 cases and found a correlation of $+.70$ between high school and college grades corrected by the Yates and Pidgeon procedures. Although we regard this as a relatively crude procedure, it seemed to work almost as well for this small sample as our more complex procedures.

One of the major advantages of the Aptitude Method is that each school or college can determine its own scale. Using the aptitude test results, which have been obtained on the school's students, a competent statistician can very quickly translate the grades into scale values using either the mean or the regression technique. If an association or group would agree on a national scale such as one with a mean of 50 and a standard deviation of 10, each school or college could determine the appropriate values for its own grade averages. This would eliminate the need for the large central organization required by the Internal Method and would enable each school or college to report its own scale value by such a simple advice as printing it as explanatory material on the transcript or informing college admissions officers and school guidance workers by some simple method of reporting. Although the regression technique is somewhat more difficult to compute than the mean technique, we would recommend it because it reduces the likelihood of error arising from small samples at any one grade level. If the computational problems present difficulties for personnel in the schools or colleges, it should be possible for some organization to take on the task of doing the necessary statistical work and reporting the results to the schools and colleges.

The Aptitude Method need not be dependent on a single aptitude test. If different aptitude tests are used, they can be equated. Thus, if four or five different scholastic aptitude tests are used by different schools or colleges they can be approximately equated by the use of appropriate norms and data already available in the literature. The Aptitude Method would work best if all the students were tested at the same point in their academic career—perhaps toward the end of the senior year in high school or just prior to admission to college. Furthermore, it would be most useful if a single national grade scale could be agreed upon. The secondary school and college scale would be similar. Since the primary use of the scale would be for the prediction of college grades, the scale values for a particular school should be based on the students from that school who complete one year of college. If possible, several years of aptitude and grade data should be used to set the first scale values for a school with annual or bi-annual corrections thereafter.

The Achievement Method

Although the Aptitude Method works relatively well, it is dependent on the scholastic aptitude of students. It is quite possible for a school or college to have relatively high aptitude students and not provide an educational program up to the capabilities of the students. On the other hand it is possible for a school or college to have a relatively low aptitude group of students and still provide a very good educational program for these students. The Aptitude Method emphasizes the aptitude students bring to the school or college rather than the quality of the education the students receive.

A criterion that might better reflect the quality of the educational program in the scaling of grades is an achievement test or battery of achievement tests. Achievement tests are intended to appraise the outcomes of instruction rather than the aptitudes students bring to the school. The Achievement Method thus makes the assumption that the level of the students' educational development as measured by an achievement test is an appropriate criterion for scaling grades. It is assumed that the achievement tests used are appropriate to the objectives of instruction of the school or college.

There is considerable evidence that schools and colleges vary greatly in the level of attainment of their students as measured by achievement tests. Learned and Wood (1938) reported great differences among high schools and colleges in a study of secondary and higher education in Pennsylvania.

They found some colleges to be so different that the top college sophomore in one college was at about the same point on the achievement tests as the lowest college sophomore in another college. Bloom (1956), and Davenport and Remmers (1950) reported great differences in achievement when the different states are compared at the high school or college levels. The 1957 Supplement to College Board Scores No. 2 (Fishman, 1957, p. 23), listed the C.E.E.B. achievement test scores made by boys in liberal arts colleges. The mean scores of the highest and lowest college groups reported are shown in the table:

	HIGH COLLEGE		LOW COLLEGE	
	Mean Score	Percentile	Mean Score	Percentile
English Composition	683	96	447	31
Social Studies	661	94	443	26
French	664	94	364	10
Biology	639	91	435	26
Chemistry	709	98	443	29
Physics	705	98	440	28
Intermediate Mathematics	697	98	448	43
Advanced Mathematics	746	99	483	43

There is little doubt that the gross differences in achievement test performances illustrated in the above table are related to differences in grading standards.

In the work on the Achievement Method, we have employed the C.E.E.B. Achievement Examinations as the criterion. Since we were concerned with total grade average rather than with grades in a single subject, we selected only students from the N.R.O. sample who had taken two or more of the C.E.E.B. Achievement Tests. This, of course, was not entirely adequate since the grade average was based on a large number of grades earned in many different fields and the achievement examination scores were available for only a few of these subject fields. It is likely that there were many gaps between the fields represented in the achievement test scores and the subject fields on which grades were assigned.

The number of students who had two or more achievement tests in our N.R.O. sample for the year 1956 was only 1,359. This is less than three-fourths of the population used in the Aptitude Method and perhaps introduces some bias in the sample. The mean technique described on page 60 was used in scaling both school and college grade averages. The correlation between the adjusted grade averages was $+.65$. However, when we applied the same corrections to the grades received by students in these schools and colleges five years previously (1951), the correlation between corrected grade averages was only $+.51$. This is about the same value as the uncorrected correlation between school and college grades in 1951.

This suggests that the Achievement Method, as we have used it, is not sufficiently stable to warrant its use. It is possible that the small sample of students available and the rather small number of achievement tests taken by these students may be responsible for the relatively low correlations obtained by the use of this scaling method. On theoretical educational grounds the Achievement Method should be as good or even superior to the Aptitude Method. The fact that it does not yield as good results should be taken as an indication that further study is needed of this method under more favorable circumstances. Unfortunately, we do not have the necessary data for a more comprehensive study of this method. McClelland's (1942) research made use of both aptitude and achievement criteria. He found the achievement criteria superior to the aptitude criteria.

Additional Relationships

We have been interested in the relationships between the Scholastic Aptitude Test scores and the different methods of scaling grades. The Internal Method applied to secondary school grade averages correlated +.57 with Scholastic Aptitude Test scores, while the Internal Method applied to college grade averages correlated +.51 with Scholastic Aptitude Test scores. It is evident that the relationship between grades scaled by the Internal Method and aptitude test scores is only slightly higher than the correlations reported in the literature between uncorrected grades and aptitude test scores. This fact has some value for admission purposes since aptitude tests can be used as a supplement to high school grades scaled by the Internal Method just as they are now used in connection with unscaled high school grades.

We also determined the multiple correlation between college grades (Internal Method) and a combination of the high school grades (Internal Method) plus Scholastic Aptitude Test scores. This multiple correlation (R) was +.74. Although this multiple correlation is only +.02 higher than the simple correlation between high school and college grades scaled by the Internal Method (+.72), it does seem to us that both the high school grades (corrected by the Internal Method) and aptitude test scores should be used in making decisions about college admission. Two independent pieces of evidence are better than one in reaching decisions as important as the admissibility of a particular student. While we would place greatest reliance on the high school grades corrected by the Internal Method, we would recommend the use of an aptitude test as a check on the grades as well as a source of evidence about characteristics of the student that may be somewhat independent of high school grades. When the two pieces of evidence check with each other, the admissions officer or high school counselor may be confident of his conclusion. When the two pieces of evidence are at variance with each other, additional evidence may be needed to explain or reconcile the conflicting evidence.

We studied the Aptitude Method (regression technique) in the same way. The correlations between the Scholastic Aptitude Test and the high school grades (corrected by the Aptitude Method) and between the Scholastic Aptitude Test and the college grades (corrected by the Aptitude Method) were +.71 and +.73 respectively. These relationships are considerably higher than the correlations between the Scholastic Aptitude Test and uncorrected high school grades (+.48) and uncorrected college grades (+.40) found with this sample of students. It is not surprising that these correlations should be so much increased since the Aptitude Method does realign grades so as to maximize the relation with scholastic aptitude test scores.

The multiple correlation between college grades (Aptitude Method) and a combination of the high school grades (Aptitude Method) plus the Scholastic Aptitude Test scores was +.80. This is something of an improvement over the correlation between high school grades (Aptitude Method) and college grades (Aptitude Method) which was +.75.

Thus, on statistical grounds as well as on grounds of confidence in reaching decisions, we see considerable value in using both an aptitude test and scaled high school grades for the prediction of college achievement.

3

Application of Scaling Procedures

to Specific Schools, Colleges,

and Subject Fields

IN CHAPTER 2 WE DE-
scribed in some detail the methods used in scaling grade
point averages. The results reported were for large samples
of students taken from as many as 125 schools and 300
colleges. In that chapter we were concerned with the relative
effectiveness of the different methods. In this chapter we will
consider the application of scaling procedures to specific
schools, colleges, and subject fields. In Chapters 4 and 5 we
will further develop the ways in which these methods may
be used at the high school and college levels.

How well do the scaling methods work for specific schools

and for specific colleges? In order to answer this question, we applied the scaling procedures to the grade point averages of students in twenty-three schools and thirteen colleges. We determined the effectiveness of the Internal and Aptitude Methods by comparing correlations derived from them with the correlations based on uncorrected grades. We did not try to apply the Achievement Method because we do not feel that our data for this method are adequate.

Application of Scaling Procedures to Specific Schools

The twenty-three schools selected had at least thirty seniors who had completed one year of college in 1957-58. Since our scaling procedures were developed on the 1955-56 college entrants from the N.R.O. population, we applied the procedures to the students from these twenty-three schools who were college entrants in 1957. That is, the scaling procedures were developed on the basis of one sample and applied to a new sample of students. This constitutes a type of cross-validation that is especially necessary in prediction research. For each school we applied the scaling procedures *only* to the college grade averages of the students from that school. That is, the school grade averages are the original grade averages received by the students, while the college grade averages for these students have been adjusted by our scaling procedures.

In Table 10, the schools are listed by code number. For each school, the table includes the correlation between the original school grade averages and the uncorrected college grade average, the correlation between the original school grade averages and the college grade averages adjusted by the Internal Method, and the correlations between the original school grade averages and college grade averages adjusted by the Aptitude Method. The schools are listed in the order of size of correlation for the Internal Method. In addition, the means and standard deviations are listed for the high school grades.

The median correlation between the uncorrected school-college grades for this group of schools is +.54 as contrasted with the median correlation on the Aptitude Method corrections of +.68 and Internal Method corrections of +.77. These correlations may be compared with the correlation of +.40 found in this study between the C.E.E.B. SAT scores and freshman college grade averages.* Another figure for contrast is the median correlation of +.41 cited in Chapter 1 † between C.E.E.B. SAT verbal scores and first-year college grade averages (Fishman, 1957, p. 7-8). There is little doubt that in general the correlations using adjusted grades are higher than those based on uncorrected college grades. Further, the evidence is clear that high school grades are better predictors of college grades (uncorrected or corrected) than are aptitude test scores.

In terms of prediction of college grades, the Internal Method of adjusting grades is superior to the uncorrected grades in all except one school. Furthermore, the Internal Method is equal or superior to the Aptitude Method in two-

* See p. 69.
† See p. 22.

thirds of the schools. It is striking that correlations of $+.80$ or higher are attained in one-fourth of the schools, while only three out of the twenty-three schools have correlations less than $+.65$. For this sample of schools, the Internal Method yields correlations which are very high—a level of relationship rarely encountered in educational prediction and research.

Table 10—Correlations Between High School Grades and College Grades for a Selected Sample of Schools

SCHOOL	NUMBER OF CASES	HIGH SCHOOL GRADE		CORRELATIONS BETWEEN SCHOOL GRADES AND:		
		Mean	Standard Deviation	College Grades (Uncorrected)	College Grades (Internal Method)	College Grades (Aptitude Method)
1	31	2.18	.79	.73	.88	.87
2	31	2.33	.89	.85	.87	.87
3	31	2.10	.57	.68	.82	.71
4	31	1.70	.76	.77	.81	.68
5	65	2.05	.74	.72	.80	.66
6	37	2.95	.69	.84	.80	.68
7	106	2.89	.50	.57	.79	.58
8	36	2.06	.56	.37	.79	.83
9	55	2.65	.40	.43	.78	.79
10	111	2.54	.48	.68	.78	.60
11	35	2.03	.64	.65	.78	.65
12	49	2.68	.64	.72	.77	.76
13	74	2.36	.53	.54	.76	.79
14	41	2.29	.45	.44	.73	.68
15	36	1.92	.51	.12	.72	.75
16	87	3.17	.52	.59	.72	.61
17	41	2.57	.63	.51	.71	.76
18	33	2.45	.43	.35	.69	.68
19	55	2.57	.57	.47	.68	.80
20	30	2.48	.36	.49	.68	.55
21	31	2.78	.54	.45	.64	.54
22	32	2.19	.63	.49	.61	.74
23	31	2.48	.46	.26	.59	.47
Median				$+.54$	$+.77$	$+.68$

No. of Schools $= 23$

While the median correlation between uncorrected high school grades and college grades corrected by the Aptitude Method is higher than that based on uncorrected grades it is not as high as the median correlation for the Internal Method. The Aptitude Method yields higher correlations than the uncorrected grades in four-fifths of the schools. In fewer than one-third of the schools the Aptitude Method yields higher correlations than does the Internal Method. It seems likely that there will be institutional variation in the efficiency of the different methods.

Three of the schools have correlations using uncorrected grades of $+.75$ or higher. It is difficult to account for these high relationships but they do suggest that a large proportion of the students in certain of the schools are selecting colleges in which they will secure about the same relative grades as they did in high school. This may reflect the quality of the guidance program and the knowledge the students may possess about different colleges before they make their choice of a college. It may also reflect the similarity of grading standards in the school-college combinations. Whatever the explanation, the evidence is clear that the relationships between high school and college grades vary greatly from school to school.

It is of interest to note that the magnitude of the correlations, especially by the Internal Method, is roughly related to the standard deviation of the high school grades. The correlations tend to be lowest in those schools that have the least amount of variation in grade averages, while the correlations tend to be highest in the schools that have greatest variation in grade averages. Some schools tend to bunch all of their college-going students at one or two grade levels (A and B

or B and C), while other schools tend to make greater use
of the different grade levels (A, B, C, D, and even F). Our
very limited evidence suggests that there is a greater likelihood that high school grades will be more predictive of college grades if there is considerable variation in the grades
assigned to the students.

In summary then, we find in this sample of twenty-three
schools a very high relationship between the grade averages
awarded to the students in school and the corrected grades the
students received in college. With only one exception, there is
some improvement in the efficiency of prediction resulting
from the scaling procedures. Thus, at the school level there
are substantial gains in prediction resulting from the application of the methods of scaling grades, with the greatest gains
usually resulting from applying what we have termed the
Internal Method. In Chapter 4 we will describe some of the
techniques a school counselor may use in actually working
with scaled grades and will consider some of the implications
of these data for the high schools.

Application of Scaling Procedures
to Specific Colleges

In thirteen colleges N.R.O. data were available for sixty or
more students. For each of these colleges the scaling procedures were applied *only* to the high school grade averages
of the students. The college grade averages were not adjusted.
Unfortunately, because of limitations in the data available,

we had to use data based on the 1955-1956 college entrants, which is the population on which the scaling procedures were developed. As a result, this table does not represent the type of cross-validation present in Table 10 for the school samples.

In Table 11, the colleges are listed by code number; and for each college is included the correlation between uncorrected school and uncorrected college grade averages, the correlation between uncorrected college grade averages and school grade averages corrected by the Internal Method, and the correlation between uncorrected college grade averages and school grade averages corrected by the Aptitude Method. For purposes of comparison, the correlations between college grades and the C.E.E.B. Scholastic Aptitude Test Scores are also included. In addition, the mean and standard deviations of the college grade averages are shown. The colleges are listed in order of magnitude of correlation using the Internal Method.

The median correlation obtained by using the uncorrected grades is $+.57$ while the median correlation between scholastic aptitude scores and college grades is $+.46$. This sample illustrates the point made in Chapter 1 that high school grades generally correlate higher with college grades than do aptitude test scores. In contrast with these two correlations are the median correlations of $+.58$ obtained by using the Aptitude Method and $+.68$ obtained by using the Internal Method. In terms of size of correlations, the Internal Method is superior to the uncorrected grades and the Aptitude Method in all of the colleges. In this sample of colleges the Aptitude Method does not prove to be superior to the uncorrected grades. Later research with more representative college populations may

Table 11—Correlations Between High School Grades, Aptitude Scores, and College Grades for a Selected Sample of Colleges

COLLEGE	NUMBER OF CASES	COLLEGE GRADES		CORRELATIONS BETWEEN COLLEGE GRADES AND			
		Mean	Standard Deviation	School Grades (Uncorrected)	School Grades (Internal Method)	School Grades (Aptitude Method)	S.A.T. SCORES
1	60	2.22	.69	.75	.84	.64	.57
2	76	2.33	.59	.64	.73	.52	.37
3	64	2.79	.52	.57	.72	.61	.46
4	152	2.69	.49	.64	.71	.61	.48
5	100	2.53	.44	.58	.70	.59	.39
6	122	2.83	.39	.56	.69	.61	.41
7	97	2.42	.59	.55	.68	.39	.25
8	67	2.51	.60	.57	.67	.58	.47
9	65	2.40	.62	.50	.67	.58	.29
10	112	2.66	.44	.51	.63	.61	.45
11	144	2.49	.71	.58	.61	.52	.54
12	65	2.09	.57	.57	.59	.49	.60
13	71	2.52	.61	.48	.58	.44	.61
Median				+.57	+.68	+.58	+.46

No. of Colleges = 13

determine whether this method is as good at the college level as it appears to be at the secondary level.

Although the adjustments do produce a higher level of correlation, the increase is not as great here as it is for the high schools. Probably the major reason is the fact that the college populations are more homogeneous than are the high school populations. This homogeneity is illustrated in Table 2 of Chapter 2. It is also made clear by noting that the median standard deviation for eighty-one high schools included in the N.R.O. data on the C.E.E.B. Scholastic Aptitude Test is 82 while the median standard deviation for forty-nine colleges is 67. Both of these figures may be contrasted with the standard deviation of 100 usually reported for College Board tests. The homogeneity of the colleges in contrast to the high schools may be attributed to selective admission policies on the part of the colleges and to self-selection on the part of the students. One of the implications of this is that higher correlations may be expected in colleges with the most heterogeneous populations (in terms of scholastic aptitude or previous scholastic achievement). It is interesting to note that college 2, which is a large public university, has the greatest variability of scholastic aptitude in this sample of colleges and has one of the higher correlations using the Internal Method.

Another possible explanation for the lower correlations at the college level in contrast to the high schools is the representatives of the sample of students for each school or college. The N.R.O. data is almost complete for the students in each high school. In fact, the basis for the collection of data is the list of graduates from each high school who went on to college. This means that the secondary schools are very adequately represented. On the other hand, the sample for each college in Table 11 represents less than one-tenth of the entering freshmen in that college. Although we have no way of determining the representativeness of these samples, we are convinced that a larger sample is needed to develop the scale values for each college and to appraise the effectiveness of the different methods in that college.

The variation in the magnitude of the correlations between uncorrected college grades and high school grades corrected by the Internal Method is related to the variability of the students (with respect to scholastic aptitude). The colleges with the most heterogeneous student populations have the highest correlations while the colleges with the most homogeneous student populations have the lowest correlations. Unlike the high school grades, the variability of the college grades does not appear to be related to the magnitude of the high school–college grade correlations. This suggests that the scaling methods are likely to be of greatest value to colleges with the greatest student variation (with respect to scholastic aptitude), although they should prove to be of considerable value to most colleges.

In summary then, we find that the correcting of school grades by the Internal Method produces considerable improvement in the relationship between school grades and college grades. However, the scaling methods do seem to work somewhat better for predicting from the high school's point of view than for predicting from the college's point of view. The differences among the colleges in level of correlations appears to be in part a reflection of the variation in the scholastic aptitude of the student populations.

Application of Scaling Procedures to Specific Subjects

So far, we have been dealing with over-all grade averages in high schools and colleges. We have regarded these grade averages as very valuable data because they represent the summing of many judgments. At the high school level, the four-year grade average represents the summing of sixteen or more judgments, while at the college level about eight or more judgments are included in the freshman grade average. Although the independence of these judgments cannot be determined, the bias of individual teachers is likely to be reduced by the averaging of many grades.

More from curiosity than from anything else, we tried scaling grades in different subjects to determine whether the scaling procedures would improve the relation between school and college grades in each subject field. We considered creating a different scale for each subject but soon recognized the complexity that this would bring about if each student's record had to be appraised with a series of scales. It seemed to us that if the over-all scale for grade averages could be applied to the grades in each field the results could be used more easily by school and college personnel.

Since the Internal Method has yielded the best results, we applied the Internal scale values for the over-all grade average in each school and college to the students' grades in each of five fields. We selected a sample from the 1957 college entrants for this purpose and found the correlation between the corrected high school and corrected college grades in each subject field. In Table 12, these fields are arranged in order of correlation between scaled school and college grades. It will be noted that the median correlation between the uncorrected grades in school and college for the different fields is +.43, a figure somewhat lower than the +.50 found for uncorrected grade averages in school and college. The median of the correlations on the corrected grades (using the Internal Method) is +.56, which is some improvement over the correlations between uncorrected grades.

Table 12—Correlations Between High School and College Grades in Selected Subject Fields

Subject Field	Number of Cases	Correlation Between Uncorrcted School and College Grades	Number of Cases	Correlation Between School and College Grades Corrected by the Internal Method
English	951	+.43	914	+.61
Mathematics	463	+.50	453	+.59
Social Sciences	835	+.43	824	+.56
Foreign Languages	623	+.36	635	+.51
Sciences	754	+.44	767	+.47
Median		+.43		+.56

The difference in the correlations for the five subject fields is somewhat difficult to explain. English and mathematics yield the highest correlations (+.61 and +.59). It is possible that there is a great deal of similarity in the types of learning in these fields at both the school and the college level and that the kinds of judgments about students made by teachers in these subject fields at the school and college level are very similar. At the other end, the low correlations between grades in school and college science may be attributed to several causes. The nature of science subject matter is likely to be quite different in schools and colleges. Furthermore, the science grade averages in school and college may represent somewhat different things for each school and student. We have put together such different courses as chemistry, botany, physics, biology, etc. Furthermore, we have not distinguished between science grades in general courses and science grades in specific subjects. Thus, the science grades may represent somewhat different types of learning and different types of judgments at the school and college levels.

Although the correlations are not high enough to permit very precise prediction of the grades students will make in particular subject fields, we do regard these correlations as high enough to justify the use of the grades in the subject fields as useful evidence in counseling students with regard to possible major fields. Incidentally, we did a small pilot study to determine whether the correlations would be higher if separate grading scales were developed for each subject. We found that the over-all correction yielded as high correlations as the special corrections for each subject field. However, we believe that further research must be done before this question is finally settled. In general, we find some promise that scaling procedures will improve the usefulness of not only over-all grade averages, but also the grades in particular subject fields. The promise is sufficient to warrant further research in this area.

4

Development of State or National
Academic Prediction Scales

Characteristics of the Scales

IT WOULD BE POSSIBLE TO represent adjusted grades by the use of a numerical scale (A = 40, B = 30, C = 20, D = 10, F = 0), or by the use of letters with + and —, such as A+, A, A—, B+, B, B—, etc. However, such scales do not lend themselves to easy interpretation and statistical manipulation, nor do they make full use of the possibilities of Academic Prediction Scales. We propose the use of a derived score with a mean of 50 and a standard deviation of 10. That is, the mean school or college grade for a large sample of students (conceivably all students in schools and colleges) would be 50. We have applied this quantitative scale to our Internal Method adjustments at both the school and college level.

We have translated the corrected grades of the 4,519 students in our 1955-56 population in the N.R.O. study into this derived score scale. The distribution of grades approximates a normal distribution as shown in Chart 3. Using the table of values for a normal distribution, we have indicated

CHART 3

Distribution of High-School Grade Point Average
in Relation to the Academic Prediction Scale

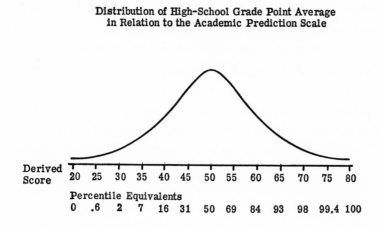

| Derived Score | 20 | 25 | 30 | 35 | 40 | 45 | 50 | 55 | 60 | 65 | 70 | 75 | 80 |

Percentile Equivalents
0   .6   2   7   16   31   50   69   84   93   98   99.4   100

the percentile equivalents for each derived score value. The college Academic Prediction Scale would have the same distribution characteristics.

The A.P.S. in this form permits one to determine where an individual student stands with respect to some large distribution of students, such as the high school or college students in the entire state or nation. It also permits the placement of a group of students in relation to a state or national distribution. This placement can be used to identify students who should be encouraged to attend college even though they do not plan to do so. Thus, students with A.P.S. scores of 65 or higher are in the upper 7 per cent of high school graduates.

Such students should have little difficulty in doing successful college work in most colleges.

Students with A.P.S. scores of 50 or higher are in the upper half of high school graduates. Our data indicates that almost all of the students in some secondary schools are at this level or higher while only a few students in other secondary schools reach this level. The A.P.S. has important consequences for regulations by some state universities which provide for the admission of students in the upper third or upper half of their graduating classes. Such regulations may have political merit, but our studies indicate that in terms of academic merit, schools and students are not so neatly divided. The A.P.S. on a state or national basis could make for marked changes in the admission and selection policies of public universities—and for major shifts in the failure rates in these institutions.

Distribution of Schools and Colleges on the Scale

Using the Internal Method we translated the grades of the schools and colleges included in our study into the Academic Prediction Scale. In Chart 4, we have shown the scale values for a sample of ten schools. The schools have been arranged from the highest to the lowest on the A.P.S. Chart 5 shows similar translations for a sample of ten colleges.

Chart 4—Academic Prediction Scale Values of Grade Point Averages for Ten Selected Schools

ACADEMIC PREDICTION SCALE SCHOOLS

Percentile	Scale Score	1	2	3	4	5	6	7	8	9	10
100	80—	A									
99.4	75—	B									
98	70—		A								
				A							
					A						
93	65—					A					
							A	A	A		
84	60—			B							
		C								A	
69	55—				B						
			B			B		B			A
				C			B				
50	50—									B	
						C					
31	45—							C			
								B		B
				D			C				
16	40—	D									
			C		C					C	
						D		D			
7	35—			F							
							D				
2	30—										C
						F				D	
								F			
0.6	25—				D						
									C		D
		F					F				
0	20—		D							F	
									D		

Chart 5—Academic Prediction Scale Values of Grade Point Averages for Ten Selected Colleges

ACADEMIC PREDICTION SCALE		COLLEGES									
Percentile	Scale Score	11	12	13	14	15	16	17	18	19	20
100	80—	A									
			A								
				A	A						
99.4	75—										
98	70—	B	B			A					
				B			A				
93	65—				B			A			
84	60—								A		
			C			B				A	
		C		C			B				
69	55—				C			B			
									B		A
50	50—					C					
							C	C			B
31	45—	D	D						C		
				D	D					B	
											C
16	40—					D		D	D		
7	35—		F	F			D				
		F									D
2	30—				F				F	C	
								F			F
0.6	25—					F					
							F				
0	20—									D	

It will be noted that the schools and colleges vary greatly in scale values. Thus, School 1 is at a different place on the scale than School 10. The difference is so great that the "C" grade in School 1 is at a higher point than the "A" grade in School 10. It is clear that a fundamental error would be involved in any research or prediction study that treats a letter grade as though it meant the same thing for each of the schools or colleges in these samples. Since we have drawn these samples from a rather limited group of schools and colleges, we are quite certain that a sample of schools and colleges selected by chance from the nation's educational institutions would reveal much greater variation than we have demonstrated here.

Guidance of Students
with Regard to College Choice

If one attempts to relate Charts 4 and 5, the problem of guidance of a student becomes clear. Consider what is likely to happen if a student from School 8 with a grade average of B (45) is advised to go to College 12. His most probable scale value in college is about 46.* If this student goes to

---

* The predicted grade is determined by the formula:

Predicted scale score $= r_{sc} (X_s - \overline{X}_s) + \overline{Y}_c$

where $r_{sc} =$ correlation between high school and college grades

$X_s =$ student's high school A.P.S. value

$\overline{X}_s =$ mean high school A.P.S. value

$\overline{Y}_c =$ mean college A.P.S. value

In this case, if we assume a correlation of $+.75$, the substitutions are $.75 (45 - 50) + 50 = 46.25$

College 12 his most probable grade is D, while if he goes to College 19 his most probable grade is B. In this case the difference between failure and superior grades lies in the choice of college.

We have selected sixteen students from one of the schools in the N.R.O. study and recorded their actual college grades as well as their scaled college grades. Five of these students had identical over-all high school grade averages of C+, six had identical high school grade average of B—, and five had high-school grade average of B+. These sixteen students went to different colleges. In Table 13 we have arranged these students by high school grade average and then shown for each student his freshman college average and this same average scaled by the Internal Method. The original grade is shown in terms of the scale A = 4, B = 3, C = 2, D = 1, F = 0.

Table 13—Original and Scaled Grade Averages Made in School Z Shown in Relation to Original and Scaled Grades Made in College by Selected Students

	Student	Original Grade	Scaled Grade	Student	Original Grade	Scaled Grade	Student	Original Grade	Scaled Grade
Grades in School Z		2.3	41		2.8	50		3.3	57
Grades Made in	A	2.5	50	F	3.1	50	L	3.4	58
Different Colleges	B	2.3	44	G	2.8	53	M	3.2	58
	C	1.8	41	H	2.8	50	N	3.1	56
	D	1.8	38	I	2.7	53	O	2.9	56
	E	1.6	41	J	2.5	53	P	2.7	56
				K	2.2	50			
Median			41			51.5			56

It will be seen that the five students who received a C+ average (scaled value 41) in school received college grades which were scaled at 38 to 50 with a median of 41. With the exception of student A, their scaled college grades were very close to their high school scale value. However, at one college the value 44 is a C+ grade while at another college 41 is a D+ grade. Note in the second set the college grades made by students with a B— average. The top student with a college B average (3.1) has the same scaled value (50) as the bottom student with a C (2.2). What has happened is that both students have been doing college work at about the level that might have been expected of them, but each college regards this level of work in a different way. In one college it is regarded as superior work while in another college it is only passing work. If the student is not placed in a college where he can do the same standard of work he has been doing previously, or if he is not fully aware of the differences in standards, he may regard his obtained grades as indicating that he is a failing student (which he is only by virtue of the college chosen). The differences may also operate to make him believe he is an outstanding success (which he also may be by virtue of the college chosen). The careful high school guidance worker may have sufficient experience with and understanding of the variation in college standards to advise students wisely with regard to choice of college. He may help the student understand the academic standards of the college the student has chosen and what these mean for him.

However, even the most experienced and capable high school counselor may not have recent information on all the

Table 14—Probability * of Individuals with Selected Scores on the High School Academic Prediction Scale Receiving Various Scores on the College Academic Prediction Scale

High School Academic Prediction Scale	College Academic Prediction Scale													Most Probable Value
	20	25	30	35	40	45	50	55	60	65	70	75	80	
80							99+	99	95	81	56	28	10	71
75							99+	96	86	64	36	14	4	68
70						99+	98	90	73	44	29	5		64
65					99+	99	93	79	47	26	9	2		61
60				99+	99	96	84	62	33	13	3	1		57
55				99+	96	88	69	42	18	5	1			54
50			99+	98	92	76	50	24	8	2				50
45		99+	99	95	82	58	31	12	4					46
40		99+	96	86	56	38	16	4	1					43
35	99+	98	91	74	47	21	7	1						39
30	99	95	81	56	28	10	2							36
25	96	86	64	36	14	4	1							32
20	90	72	44	18	5	1								29

* (Based on an r of +.71, mean of .50, standard deviation of 10.)

colleges the students from that high school are considering. The use of scaling procedures such as these will enable the counselor to estimate the most probable college scale value for students and the probability of students receiving different college scale values. In Table 14, we have shown the high school and college A.P.S. values using a correlation of +.71. In this table it will be noted that for a high school A.P.S. value of 60, most students may be expected to have a college A.P.S. value of 45 or higher. Thirty-three per cent of the students with 60 in high school may be expected to have a value of 60 or higher in college, while 13 per cent of the students with 60 in high school may be expected to have a college A.P.S. value of 65 or more. It will be noted that for students with a high-school A.P.S. of 35, there are only seven chances in 100 of making a college A.P.S. of 50 or more, while for students with an A.P.S. of 65, there are only seven chances out of 100 of making a college A.P.S. of 50 or less.

Table 14 has been prepared for A.P.S. values on a theoretical basis assuming a mean of 50, a standard deviation of 10, and a correlation of +.71 between scaled school and scaled college grades. More specific tables may be prepared for a particular secondary school on the basis of the records for a two- or three-year period.

Having these A.P.S. values for individual students, the counselor may then consult the A.P.S. values for the colleges the student is considering to determine what grades in the different colleges are received by students with similar A.P.S. values. The counselor may also enable the student to consider other colleges where his A.P.S. value would lead to successful college achievement (C or better). Where the student wishes to attend a particular college with A.P.S. values somewhat higher than the student may be expected to achieve, the counselor may at least enable the student to recognize the academic standards he must achieve if he is to successfully complete the college. Using the grades in particular subjects as described in Chapter 3, the guidance worker may help the students recognize the differential predictions for success in the different subject fields. These differential predictions should be one source of information for the student in choosing a field of specialization.

The counselor may also use these data to identify students with great promise who should be encouraged to go to college. Since grades tend to be relatively highly correlated from year to year, the Academic Prediction Scale may be used to determine academic promise as early as the second or third year of high school so that parents, teachers, and others may become aware of college potential very early in the student's high school career. It is likely that these data may be used as a basis for helping the student select courses in high school, and as a basis for helping the student find scholarship aid or other support to attend college.

Selection of Students
for College Admission

The college admissions officer has the problem of selecting the students most likely to be successful in academic achievement in his college. While he may also be interested in personality, character, manners, etc., his major decisions are usually with reference to academic potential. Table 14 may also be used by the college admissions officer to determine the probable success of each student who applies for admission. This officer must determine the scale values for grades in his own college. Then he must apply the scale values of each school to the high school grades reported for that student. The probabilities in Table 14 are, of course, reported for a theoretical distribution of students in schools and colleges with a correlation of +.71. The admissions officer may study the results for students over a period of two or three years to determine the correlation between scaled high school grades and grades in his institution. From these data he may wish to construct a table which more accurately reflects the situation in his own college.

If the number of applicants to the college is sufficiently greater than the number of students who are actually admitted, the admissions officer using grades as well as aptitude test scores may admit only those students who are likely to receive satisfactory grades. It should be possible for the admissions officer to so select students that very few are in danger of failing. Thus, if College 15 in Chart 5 selects only students with high school A.P.S. values of 50 or higher, only a few students are likely to receive grades of less than C. If students with values of 55 or higher are selected, almost none should receive grades of less than C. In any case, the probabilities may be determined from Table 14 for any specific level. These estimates, of course, depend on the maintenance of the same academic standards in the college.

5

Use of Academic Prediction Scales

by High School Counselors

and College Admissions Officers

HIGH SCHOOL COUNSELORS
and college admissions officers may have a theoretical interest
in the improvement of academic prediction for the country as
a whole, but they have a real need to improve the academic
prediction for the students with whom they are directly concerned. Each counselor and admission officer wishes to know
where his institution stands on the scales described in this
work and whether or not the procedures described here will
improve his ability to predict the college achievement of the
students with whom he works.

97

High School Counseling

The high school counselor for college bound students has the task of helping the student select a college, helping him in tentatively considering subject areas and occupations of special interest, and helping the student become admitted to one of the colleges of his choice.

Some counselors have devoted many years to this work and have built up an experience with students and colleges that enables them to estimate with considerable accuracy what a particular student is likely to do in a particular college. Others who have had relatively little experience are not able to make very accurate estimates of the capabilities of a student or the demands and requirements of a college. Even counselors with considerable experience may have difficulty in making estimates for the increasing range of colleges their students desire to enter. Furthermore, the counselor with experience has difficulty in communicating to new counselors the wisdom he has acquired over the years.

As we study the data provided by the National Registration Office on schools and colleges we find some schools have so placed their students in college that almost every student has done C or better work in college. Other schools have a somewhat poorer record for their students in college. We are of the opinion that the differences in performance of students in college are largely a function of the choice of college for each student. This opinion is supported by the evidence in Table 10 in Chapter 3 of the variation in correlations between uncorrected grades in schools and colleges. Thus School 4 in this table has a correlation of +.77 between uncorrected school and college grades, while School 8 has a correlation of only +.37 between uncorrected school and college grades. In terms of prediction of college achievement, it is likely that the counseling of students in School 4 was far superior to that in School 8. Since the correlations using the Internal Method of correcting grades are +.81 and +.79 for these two schools, it is evident that the grades in both schools are sufficiently accurate to permit of almost equally precise predictions of college grades.

The counselors in most schools should, by the use of academic prediction data, be able to make as accurate estimations of the college achievement of their students as is now done by the most experienced and capable counselors. In effect, the use of systematic evidence in the prediction of academic achievement should enable each school to do as good a job of placing students in college as is now done by the school with the most informed counseling staff.

Ideally, academic prediction scales should be set up by organizations that can bring together the data from many high schools and colleges within a state or within a larger geographical region. Such an organization, staffed by statistical experts using modern high-speed computers, could do much more accurate and precise scaling than is possible for an individual high school counselor. The development of academic prediction scales by state or national organizations may not come about for many years, if at all. The high school counselor can, nevertheless, make some use of scaling procedures with the data at present available.

The counselor might begin by assembling the records of his graduates who entered college. Three to five years of such records might be assembled, depending upon the number of cases involved. Ideally, at least 100 cases should be used in this study. For each student, the counselor should determine his high school grade average, his first-year college average, and his scholastic aptitude score. In most of the work on the N.R.O., we have employed a scale of 4 = A, 3 = B, 2 = C, 1 = D, 0 = F, to quantify the school and college grades.

Once the necessary data have been collected, the counselor might work out the relationship between the uncorrected high school and college grade averages. We have found a scatterplot very helpful for this purpose. A typical high school–college grade average scatterplot is shown in Chart 6.* Here the high school averages are shown along one side while the college grade averages are shown along the other side. Each tally represents a student and shows the high school and college grade average for this student. At this point the counselor might compute the product moment correlation between school and college grade averages. Several references for the computation of correlation coefficients are the following: Garrett, 1947; Guilford, 1950; McNemar, 1949; Walker, 1943. The correlation coefficient for the data in Chart 6 is +.54.

It may help the counselor to mark off some arbitrary set of upper and lower limits for predicting college grade averages from high school grade averages. In Chart 6 we have marked off an upper limit of half a grade (+.5) above the

* The decimal point has been dropped in the grade averages.

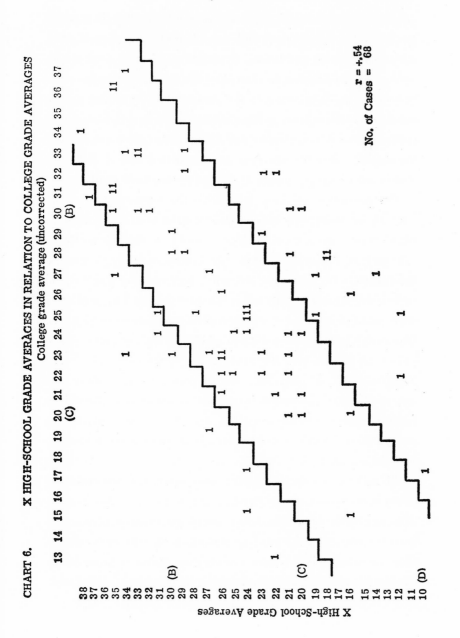

CHART 6.   X HIGH-SCHOOL GRADE AVERAGES IN RELATION TO COLLEGE GRADE AVERAGES

original high school grade and a lower limit of half a grade
(—.5) below the original high school grade. Although this is a
very arbitrary set of limits, it rather quickly gives a rough
picture of the relationship between the two set of grades. One
can get a crude picture of the relationship by counting the
number of tallies outside these limits. For Chart 6, forty-three
tallies are within the limits and twenty-five tallies are outside
the limits. Thus 63 per cent of the tallies (43 ÷ 68) are
within the arbitrary limits of + and — one-half grade.

The counselor might now turn to the organization of the
data by colleges. He may find that groups of five or more
students have gone from his high school to particular colleges.
For each of these sub-groups, the counselor may inspect the
relationship between the students' high school grades and
their college grades. Table 2 in Chapter 2 is an illustration of
such relationships for the high school represented in Chart 6.
One can determine the extent to which the high school–college
grades are in roughly the same order within each sub-group.
Thus in Table 2, only four out of twenty-eight students are
out of order. This rough inspection suggests that there is a
higher relationship between this school's grades and college
grades than is represented by the scatterplot shown in Chart 6
and the correlation of +.54.

At this point, the counselor may wish to determine the
effect of various techniques of adjusting grades. The simplest
(but probably least effective) technique is to make a subjective estimate of the grading standards of different colleges.
One or more high school counselors might independently
divide a list of colleges into three or more groups on the basis

of what they know about the colleges. Group 1 might consist
of the colleges with lowest grading standards, group 2 could
include colleges with average grading standards, and group 3
could include the colleges with the highest grading standards.
One estimate of the value of the grades for the three groups
might be to use the modified values shown in Table 7
(Chapter 2). Using these modified values, the counselor
should take each student's record in college, determine
whether the college is in group 1, 2, or 3, and then substitute the modified grade-average values for that group of
colleges for the student's actual college grade average. After
he has made these substitutions in all the student records the
counselor may construct another scatterplot to determine the
relationship between the high school grade averages and the
modified grade averages. This should in most cases be substantially higher than the relationship for school grades with
uncorrected college grades.

Another approach to the scaling of grades would be to use
the Aptitude Method. Here the counselor may wish to construct a scatterplot of the relationship between high school
grades and scholastic aptitude test scores. For this scatterplot
a line may be drawn to represent the relationship between
grades and aptitude scores. This line may be interpreted as
showing the scholastic aptitude score that best represents each
grade. A more precise method would be to compute the
regression of scholastic aptitude scores on grades and to
substitute scholastic aptitude values for the grade values.

An estimation of the scaled values for selected colleges
may be made from the class descriptions being released by

some colleges. These descriptions generally include College Board Test scores, grade distributions, and other information (College Board Review, 1959, p. 2). It is likely that these class profiles will be available for additional colleges in the future.

Where the class description provides both the distribution of grades and the College Board Scholastic Aptitude Test scores, it is possible to roughly estimate the aptitude values for the grades in that college. This may be done by using a regression method where it is assumed that the average correlation between college grade and aptitude test score is +.50. An even rougher approximation may be made by substituting the aptitude distribution for the grade distribution in each college.

Once the aptitude adjustments are determined for each college it is possible to substitute for each student's grade average the appropriate aptitude value for that grade in that college. Once again the student's grade average in high school (with or without the high school's aptitude correction) may be correlated with the student's grade average in college corrected by this rough aptitude method.

Further refinements in scaling grades must await either an exchange of data between schools and colleges in which a standard set of procedures is used or the development of academic prediction scales through state or national organizations. It will probably be necessary for any organization undertaking these scaling procedures to begin with data on each school or college for the previous three to five years. These results would make clear the level of improvement in prediction to be gained by the scaling procedures.

Once a scheme of scaling grades is set up, each counselor will have the scale value of the grades in his school, the scale values for the grades in most of the colleges to which his school sends students, and the scholastic aptitude test results. Using probability tables such as Table 14 (Chapter 4), it will be possible to determine the most probable scaled grades each student is likely to receive in college and the general limits within which he may be expected to receive scaled grades. Then, for each of the colleges for which scaled grades are available (see Chart 5, Chapter 4), it will be possible to estimate the probable grades each student is likely to receive. This will enable the counselor to advise the student with regard to the academic level he may be likely to achieve in each college he is considering.

The counselor will, of course, take into consideration other data such as the student's aptitude scores, his interests, background, aspirations, choice of career and field of specialization, as well as other relevant information available in the school records and the observations of various persons who have known the student for some time. The academic prediction scale plus the aptitude scores are likely to form the primary basis for estimating the probability of the student's doing acceptable levels of academic work. Other data may be useful in determining how well the student is likely to fit into the college environment.

College Admissions

The college admissions officer faces problems very similar to those of the high school counselor. He wishes to select students who can fit into his institution and who can meet the academic requirements of the college or university. He wishes to decrease the proportion of failing students and increase the proportion of passing students.

If the admissions officer has had a great deal of experience with the schools that send students to his institution, he may have developed his ability to interpret transcripts and other data in the light of what he knows about each school. He may even have developed a very systematic set of procedures for adjusting school grades by methods such as those used by Burnham (1959) at Yale University. The inexperienced admissions officer may have some difficulty in interpreting transcripts and other data unless his predecessors have built up a very systematic procedure which can be passed on. Both experienced and inexperienced admissions officers may have difficulty if their institution draws students from a large number of schools or if there are many changes in the schools from which the college draws students.

Here again the ideal solution for the use of Academic Prediction Scales would be for central agencies to accumulate the data for many schools and colleges and to process the data in such a way that it could be efficiently used by both schools and colleges. Until such procedures are developed, the individual admissions officer must do the best he can with the data available.

Perhaps the most direct attack on the problem would be to use the methods described by Burnham (1959). He found that one group of schools sent sizeable numbers of students to Yale over a period of years. For these schools he developed methods of adjusting high school grades that made them excellent predictors (correlation of $+.76$) of Yale freshman grades. These procedures made it possible to use some of the student records with considerable precision even though other records could not be treated with the same confidence.

A larger number of schools' records could be handled with equal precision if admissions officers for several institutions would pool their data and process such data by the Burnham procedures or by the use of the Aptitude Method described in Chapter 2.

A less accurate method would be to divide high schools roughly into about three groups on the basis of subjective estimates of their grading standards. Group 1 would be the schools with the lowest grading standards, group 2 would be the schools with average grading standards, and group 3 would be the schools with the highest grading standards. Values like those in Table 7 of Chapter 2 might be used as a rough substitute for the actual grades on the students' transcripts from each group of schools. The relationship between the adjusted high school grades and the college freshmen grades could be compared with the relationship between the uncorrected high school grades and the college freshmen grades to determine the effect of the adjustments.

The basic problem in all of these scaling methods is to secure enough data from each school or group of schools to make a reliable estimate of the grading standards of each school. The National Registration Office procedures make all the data available for each of the member schools. Unfortunately, it provides data for only about 125 schools. It is conceivable that high schools might be persuaded to release the types of data now available in the class descriptions provided by some colleges (College Board Review, 1959, p. 2). If this were done, it would be possible to make adjustments to school grades by the use of the Aptitude Method.

It is, of course, assumed that the admissions officer will make use of aptitude test results as well as other data in making decisions about individual students. The procedures involved in utilizing a variety of types of data have been developed in workshops for admissions officers sponsored by the College Entrance Examination Board. Such procedures are also described by Dyer and King (1955). Table 14 in Chapter 4 is an illustration of one of the procedures by which the admissions officer can make decisions on a probability basis.

The admissions officers has the responsibility of keeping his faculty informed when the admissions procedures are altered. If the admissions officer is able to predict college grades with greatly increased accuracy and if he selects only those students who are likely to do successful academic work in his institution, the faculty may want to make some provision to maintain a consistent set of academic standards. Each shift in selection procedures may produce no changes in failing ratios if the faculty merely continues to fail the same proportion of students without regard to level of academic performance.

6

Conclusions and Implications

AS A RESUUT OF LOOKING AT THE high school and college grades for a large sample of students, schools, and colleges, we found more consistency in achievement patterns than is generally recognized. Indeed, our findings suggest that there is almost as much consistency between high school and college grades as there is among grades within a single institution. That is, the level of correlation coefficients we found, the correlations of $+.72$ and $+.75$ that emerged from the application of the Internal and Aptitude Methods respectively, are close to the relationship between first- and second-term grades (about $+.80$) within colleges. The correlations found here begin to approximate the limits of our present grading procedures.

We cannot overemphasize the fact that what we have found

and have reported here is not a new variable in human behavior nor a new index to academic achievement. This striking relationship between high school and college grades has long been obscured because grades have been treated as if they were equivalent irrespective of the institutions in which they were earned. Many admissions officers and high-school guidance counselors have been wiser than the researchers who were looking for better predictions. The admissions officers and counselors have long used formal and informal methods of considering institutional variation. What our research has demonstrated is that such methods can be systematized and codified and thus used more efficiently and more broadly.

The meaning and possible uses of Academic Prediction Scales raise a host of important practical, theoretical, and philosophic questions. They have many significant implications for educational practice, test development, and educational research. We would be remiss if we did not at least mention some of the more important problems and implications raised by this research.

Implications for College Choice and Admission: Risk versus Calculated Risk

Someone once said that there is a college for every student. At face value, this clearly overstates the case. However, there is much evidence in our data and elsewhere to support the view that a large proportion of college failures and drop-outs are the result of students (at least in the first year of college) choosing the wrong college. It seems clear to us that many college failures are not a matter of personal inadequacy for college work in some absolute sense.

The student who chooses a college for which he is unprepared or ill-equipped can hope for little but frustration and failure. The college that accepts students who are ill-suited to meet its demands and standards must expect a large proportion of failures and drop-outs. Such failures * constitute costly errors for everyone concerned.

Some students do know what the odds are against them, and they know that they can hope to meet their college's demands only by strenuous and consistent effort. Even so, they consider the risk worth taking. Some of these students fail, and some may become outstanding scholars. Some students, although well prepared to undertake a particular college curriculum, find their attention and effort diverted to other activities; and such students may risk failure in their studies in order to fulfill such competing demands. A college faculty may wish to modify its curriculum, or it may wish to have a more diversified student population, and it may therefore admit students who do not appear to meet the standards of its usual student body. In the course of such changes there is likely to be loss: some of the new courses may succeed, some may not come up to expectations; some of the new

---

* Our attention has been called to the possibility that college failure may not represent total failure. Even the student who fails out of college may have learned a great deal while in college and may have profited from the experience. While we do regard this as a possibility, we are of the opinion that college success is preferable to college failure and that the student may learn more if he completes several years of college than if he attends a year or less. We do not see much that is good in a student's failing out of college when the choice of a different college might have meant successful completion of a program of studies.

student groups may be successful, some may fail or drop out. College losses or student failures that result from circumstances such as these cannot rightly be called errors. They may be more appropriately thought of as the cost of risk-taking.

We are convinced that the careful use of Academic Prediction Scales can move the general problem of academic failure from the realm of gross error closer to the realm of calculated risk. Even the best predictor does not guarantee success. The predictor does not tell the student to enter this college or some other one, nor does it decide which students should be admitted to college. The function of a good predictor is to provide evidence from which one can calculate the probabilities of success or failure, and from which one can estimate the amount of effort necessary for a cause to be won. Whether the cause is worth the risk is another matter. Whatever the predictions, the student or the college must decide whether to take the risk.

The difficulty with most predictors is that they do not yield sufficiently precise evidence to serve as a basis for decisions. Too often when a student and college think they are taking a calculated risk, they are making a gross error because of imperfections in the evidence on which the decision is based. Adjusted grades are important not because they will eliminate risk, but because they yield more accurate evidence of college potential. Their use can greatly reduce the instances of error. And, although we have treated error here largely in terms of the student who undertakes a college program in which he will fail, we believe that errors of the opposite kind are just as serious. The student who chooses a college in which he will not be challenged and where he can get by with minimal effort is, in our view, losing too. The college which selects students it is not prepared to challenge, whom it houses rather than educates, is not adding as much to the educational venture as it might.

It should be clear, then, that our findings have little direct bearing on the question of whether or not a student should select the college in which he is most likely to succeed, or on the question of whether or not a college should restrict its enrollment to students within a particular range of ability or achievement. These are crucial educational policy questions that must be decided on bases other than Academic Prediction Scale findings. At the same time, the analysis of findings derived from the use of such scaling techniques will provide important evidence about the consequences of one choice or another. Such data should also make possible a more precise implementation of whatever policy is chosen. If, for example, a college decides to bring in a more varied student population, adjusted grades may become one of the most important criteria to consider in controlling or implementing this variation. If the college policy is to vary the population in terms of academic potential, adjusted grades should provide a reliable index to such variation. If the policy is to vary the population in terms of social background or other characteristics, adjusted grades are likely to prove useful as a basis for controlling academic potential.

Whatever use is made of Academic Prediction Scales, it must be remembered that they are simply devices for improving the prediction of one set of grades from another set of grades. Such a device places grades from schools and colleges on a quantitative scale. The quantitative scale should not be interpreted as a qualitative scale of the merits of particular educational programs. It is quite likely that the efficiency of the scales for prediction will frequently be misinterpreted as evidence that a scale is an index of the relative educational merits of different schools or colleges or of different educational curricula. We find it quite conceivable that a school that places low on the A.P.S. may be doing a more effective educational job than many schools that place higher on the scale. The qualitative characteristics of educational programs should be evaluated by determining how effectively they achieve their educational objectives. A school with one group of students may need to do a quite different educational task than a school with a very different group of students. A school or college operating within one community or educational situation may need to offer a very different set of learning experiences than a school or college within a different context. Thus, there may be many different types of educational programs that have important and meaningful qualitative differences; such differences are not reflected in a simple quantitative scale designed to maximize the predictability of academic achievement as measured by grades.

Implications for Curriculum Study
and Grading Standards:
Local Norms and National Norms

At present, the same grades and grade distributions are used both for informing the student how well he is doing in his studies in the school and as an index of his potential work in college, where he will be in a quite different group and perhaps studying under quite different circumstances. The reference group for a student's grades in school is the group of students in that school, whereas the reference group for a student's grades as an index of his college potential consists of the students from a large number of high schools. These different reference groups are clearly not identical, a fact which no doubt confuses a great many students as well as teachers and parents.

The A.P.S. can permit each school or college to have its own distribution of grades as well as to translate its distribution into a national scale. This should make it more possible for the distribution of grades in each institution to reflect the particular characteristics of that institution and of its students. The A.P.S. enables a school or college to be somewhat more free in determining its own grading characteristics than would otherwise be the case, since these local grades can be translated into a national grade scale when they are considered by other educational institutions or selecting agencies. The analogy of currency (Ward, 1959) may help to give meaning to these procedures. Thus each country has its own currency, which reflects the value of work, consumer goods, and capital resources within the country. Economic transactions and exchanges of currency across national boundaries are expedited by the setting of exchange values for currency. This enables the country to carry on its economic activity within the country, as well as with other countries. It may keep these two scales quite distinct and use each as is appropriate.

The dual scale for grading (local and A.P.S.) may be very helpful in explaining grades to students and to their parents. These two scales may also be very useful in permitting teachers and administrators to comprehend more fully the meaning and significance of their own grading procedures as well as the grading procedures of other schools and colleges. Revision of local grading procedures will eventually be reflected in the A.P.S. values for these grades. Perhaps one caution should be noted here. Merely changing the symbols or distribution of grades locally will not have a real effect on the A.P.S. values since the A.P.S. values are based on the *relationship* between local grading standards and national grading standards. Educational changes which result in greater competence in the students will bring about new values on the A.P.S.

While the A.P.S. introduces the possibility of more flexibility in grading standards within each school or college, the availability of national norms, in addition to permitting better predictions of college success, provides improved evidence for the study of local grading and educational practices. Thus, if a school is interested in how well its science courses prepare its students for college science, one source of evidence would be the grades its former students had received in college science courses. As long as the school has no basis on which to equate grades from different colleges, however, the problem of interpreting such evidence is almost impossible to resolve. The availability of A.P.S. grades makes it possible for a school to compare the science grades of students who went to different colleges, and thus to combine evidence from many sources.

Improvement of Grading Procedures

Grades are assigned by individual teachers on the basis of a great variety of evidence and according to widely different standards. Although there may be a general standard for a school or college, the standards are likely to vary considerably from teacher to teacher and from subject to subject.

The development of the A.P.S. enables the faculty within a particular school or college to give more meaning to its own grading procedures and to use the scale as one criterion for studying and checking them. If the school grades have a relatively low relationship with college grades (adjusted by the AP.S.) the school may wish to study its grading procedures to determine the possible causes of this low relationship. The same may be true in a college with respect to the relation between its grades and adjusted high school grades.

The faculty, for example, may ask whether the relationship between school and college grades is higher in some subject areas than in others. Here the A.P.S. may be used to adjust college or school grades in each subject, and then the relationship between school and college grades in each subject field may be determined. The faculty may then analyze the different relationships to determine why some are higher than others. The distributions of each set of grades within the institution may be compared with each other to determine whether the source of variation is in the different standards used by individual teachers. The reader is referred to the procedures reported by the Muskingum College Faculty (1937, pp. 267-77) for standardizing its semester grades.

If appropriate achievement tests can be found, the relationship between grades in a subject and scores on the achievement test may help to determine the extent to which grading procedures are related to other criteria of academic competence. Scholastic aptitude tests may also be related to specific grades to determine whether the grades reflect in part the scholastic ability of the students. Out of these studies, the faculty may be able to develop procedures that will improve the reliability and validity of its grading. It is likely that such improvement will come from more systematic use of evidence in grading. Such evidence may include observation of the student in class and laboratory; products of the students such as problems solved, essays, term papers, etc.; performance on quizzes and other progress tests; and performance on carefully constructed final and comprehensive examinations. Relevant standardized achievement tests may also prove helpful in improving grading procedures. The use of clear criteria for marking papers and the use of two or more independent judges may bring about considerable improvement in the accuracy of grading procedures.

The renewed emphasis placed on grades by the A.P.S. requires that every effort be made to clarify the grading procedures. This is not the place to discuss all the ways in which grading may be improved. However, every effort made to improve the precision and meaningfulness of grades will give both faculty and students more confidence in the grades. Grade reports are likely to motivate students to more intensive study and academic effort if they regard the grades as fair and precise. High school students are also likely to be motivated by the recognition that grades in school are relatively accurate predictors of grades in college and that grades are a major basis for college admission and for other academic decisions.

Grades as a Record of Experience: Status versus History

This demonstration of the consistency of the student's academic achievement at the high school and college level clearly places renewed importance on high school grades as predictors of college potential. In effect, the A.P.S. operates on the thesis that if we know the past academic history of the student we can predict what he will do in the future. There are, of course, limits to this assumption, since we are here concerned only with his grades in secondary school and we predict only his grades in his first year of college. Nonetheless, the emphasis in the A.P.S. is on the academic history of the student and of the school as the predictor of the future academic performance of the student.

In contrast, scholastic aptitude tests measure the student's ability to solve specific problems at a particular point in time and predict his future grades from his performance on the test. The tests thus start with the student's status at a particular time and predict from this evidence. It is possible for a student with a very mediocre academic history to perform very well on a test, and his test performance may be given more weight than his previous history for determining his admissibility to college.

There is much that is appealing in a measure of status as an indicator of potential as contrasted with a measure derived from the history of the individual. Such a status measure in effect gives the student one more chance, while the historical measure posits a kind of determinism in that the future is tied to the past.

We do recognize that a student may be judged too leniently or too severely by his teachers in high school because of personality, background characteristics, or because of the type of interaction he has with the high school faculty. We recognize that some students may find themselves when they enter college or when they are on their own and separated from family and friends. The same variables may also be operating in a reverse way in that a student who is very successful in high school may not be equally successful in college. Thus the pressure at home that may have kept him working very well in high school may no longer be there to support him when he enters college. Loneliness in a new surrounding may prevent the student from doing as well in

college as he did in high school. The very personality characteristics that were prized in high school may be regarded
as less desirable in college.

However, the correlation of +.75 indicates that the number
of such students must be relatively small. We would expect
that fewer than 10 per cent of students would be found who
are very high on the high school A.P.S. and very low on the
college A.P.S. Even so, the fact that some students may
change sufficiently to make significant differences in academic
achievement at high school and college argues for some way
of combining a historical index with a status index. Even
though the scholastic aptitude test adds little to the multiple
correlation, it may make a difference for individuals. High
school counselors and college admissions officers are likely
to be more confident of their advice or selection if two
independent types of evidence are used in reaching an important decision about the academic career of the student. When
both the test results and the scaled grades are in agreement,
there should be little doubt about the decision. When the test
results and the scaled grades are very different, further evidence may be needed to determine which is the better predictor for the future. While the probability is in favor of the
scaled grades, we would urge that high school counselors
and college admissions officers consider all the relevant information before coming to a decision. A record should be
maintained of such cases and follow-up information gathered
to determine the validity of the decision as one basis for
future decisions.

Another problem posed by the A.P.S. is the extreme student. The scaled values assigned to high school or college

grades are based on previous experience with an entire group of students. The A.P.S. makes use of the correlations between high school and college grades and relates the variation and central tendency of a group to this correlation. However, it is possible that the extreme student at the top of a particular distribution may really be much better than the scaled score assigned to him, while the extreme student at the lower end of the distribution may be far poorer than the scaled score assigned to him. There is little one can do about this except to be very cautious in making decisions about the extreme 1 or 2 per cent in each distribution. There is some comfort in the thought that the student at the top extreme should do as well as or better than the scaled score would indicate and that the student at the lower extreme is likely to do no better than the scaled score would indicate. Decisions about these extreme students will most likely be aided by reference to scholastic aptitude tests or other evidence.

Implications for Testing:
Test Validation

Achievement tests are frequently validated against teachers' grades within a school or college. The availability of the A.P.S. permits the validation of a test against a larger and more varied sample of students. If the local teachers' grades are translated into the A.P.S. values, it is possible to combine student groups from several schools or colleges and to relate the test results to this more varied sample of students and schools. Peters (1952) found the correlation between selected achievement test scores and grades (corrected by an Aptitude Method) significantly higher than the correlation between the same test scores and uncorrected grades.

The A.P.S. may also be used to determine whether the achievement test discriminates effectively at all levels of student achievement. These data should provide a basis for improving the discrimination of the test at appropriate levels. Thus, if there are particular levels where the test does not effectively discriminate among students, additional work may be done to find test items and scoring procedures that will make the test more discriminating. It may be found that several quite different tests are needed to secure discrimination at all the different levels.

The use of the scale also permits and encourages the development of achievement tests that bridge the school and college years. This should encourage the development of a battery of tests that cover the twelfth and thirteenth years of schools, since grades at either or both high school and college can be put into the same scale for validation purposes. The striking variation among schools and colleges revealed by the scale suggests that the students in some schools may be so far advanced over students in other schools that tests intended for students who have completed thirteen years of school may be appropriate for high-school seniors (twelfth year of school) in some schools, while tests intended for high school juniors (eleventh year of school) may be appropriate for high school seniors in other schools. The Advanced Placement Program of the College Entrance Examination Board (1956) is a step in this direction, since it enables high school seniors to demonstrate the equivalent of a year of college work in a subject.

In selecting populations of students for test validation studies, schools or colleges with careful and accurate grading procedures may be combined with schools and colleges with less accurate grading procedures. The use of the scales and data on the relations between school and college grades should permit the selection of schools or colleges with grades highly related to achievement at another level. The validation studies may thus deliberately include schools or colleges with grading procedures of a known validity (i.e., relation with grades at another level of education). The scales also permit the more careful selection of student samples for norming purposes. Schools or colleges may be selected because their students fall in a particular segment of the grade distribution. The scales should also be useful in selecting equivalent populations at different times and as a basis for establishing the equivalence between two sets of norms.

Implications for Testing:
Criterion Analysis

The research reported here raises a rather fundamental question about test methodology. It begins with the rather simple notion that the best prediction of what a student will do in the future is the evidence of what he has done in the past. More particularly, it takes the view that the best predictor of academic grades in the future is the history of the student's previous academic grades. The basic problem then becomes how the previous history of the student can be best summarized and codified so that it can be utilized for the prediction.

The test worker who makes use of the underlying notion in this research will approach the problem of prediction in a somewhat different from that which prevails at present. He will analyze what behavior and achievement the grade requires and the means by which students can attain them. He will then attempt to determine the opportunities in the student's previous history to satisfy similar criteria or to attain similar goals in the past. The analysis of these should then suggest testing procedures that most nearly tap these same experiences and history of the past. For example, it would be possible to include in a test a complex learning task in which each examinee must learn something new; the speed, accuracy, and complexity of the learning may be determined from the responses he gives to the test. If such a learning task is related to the kinds of learning the student will have to do in college or the kinds of learning he has been expected to do in the past, the relationship to previous or later learning may be expected to be quite high.

In the following section we have suggested some new areas of concentration for testing. Here we mean only to suggest the need for different ways of viewing the problem so that testers may break through the very strong boundaries the pioneers in the field of testing have created by their very powerful instruments and methods—which may now be less relevant to the problems of education than they were three or four decades ago. Other directions are suggested by the assessment methodologies that attempt to relate personality, attitudes, interests, and cognitive abilities to the specific demands of the environment. Although such methods are still quite complex and expensive, they do suggest procedures that in the long run may be more valuable than some of the simpler quantitative procedures now used. It is likely that the assessment procedures will also become simpler and easier to use in the future.

Implications for Testing: The Need for New Tests

After almost fifty years of research and development, the average correlation between scholastic aptitude tests and college achievement is of the order of $+.50$, a figure that has not significantly changed from the correlation of $+.49$ between aptitude tests and college achievement reported by Jordan (1920) in 1920. Thus, in almost half a century of major research and development we have not materially improved our effectiveness in the prediction of academic achievement. In contrast is the correlation of $+.75$ reported here between scaled high school and college grades. It is true that the multiple correlation of scholastic aptitude and scaled high school grades with scaled college grades is $+.80$. The scholastic aptitude test still contributes to the prediction of college grades, although the contribution is relatively small.

If the A.P.S. is used, it may do much to remove the likelihood that a given student will fail—if he is placed in a college which is appropriate to his level of academic competence. The present type of scholastic aptitude test may still be of value in schools or colleges where the scaling procedures do not improve the predictions significantly. The present type of scholastic aptitude test may also be useful where the number of students going on to college from a particular school is too small to develop an adequate scale level for the school. This type of scholastic aptitude test is also likely to remain useful for scholarship selection and for selection purposes where applicants for admission are very homogeneous on the A.P.S.

However, the high levels of prediction resulting from the A.P.S. may so improve the selection of students that new types of scholastic proficiency tests will become more useful. For example, if the A.P.S. reduces the likelihood of failure sufficiently, aptitude tests will no longer be needed for weeding out potentially failing students. New aptitude tests may now be developed to select students who show a greater potential than their previous academic records demonstrate. It might be argued that this potential may be appraised by a type of test that measures learning potential, rather than a test that appraises what the student has learned in the past.

Still another use for aptitude tests might be to select among equally able students on the A.P.S. those students who are likely to become most creative and productive in the future or those students who have particular characteristics that are highly prized by a particular college or set of colleges. Pace and Stern (1958), in their study of college environments, found great differences among colleges in the behaviors and characteristics which are expected or desired by faculty and students. Some colleges emphasize the development of highly analytical reading and problem solving skills, while other colleges emphasize the accumulation of knowledge through listening to lectures and observing demonstrations. Some colleges emphasize learning from first-hand experiences and the reading of primary sources, while other colleges emphasize learning from textbooks and lectures. Perhaps it is this institutional variation that we must consider in developing the aptitude and other selection instruments for the future.

Such instruments may also be of value in identifying the student characteristics for which a particular grade is given. Is memory the most important characteristic? Verbal ability? Ability to reason? Docility? Flexibility? Independence? Thus, the question may be turned around; and, instead of being concerned about predicting grades, we may become interested in determining what the grade represents. The tests would become analytical tools rather than prediction devices. Gulliksen (1950, pp. 100-103) suggested this use of tests.

Another possible development is the use of tests to determine the student's present level of achievement as a basis for placement within the college program. Such tests may be more of the achievement rather than aptitude type and they may be designed to appraise the student's grasp of a subject and the extent to which he has achieved the complex mental processes that are important in that subject. On the basis of these tests it should be possible to determine whether the student may begin his college work with advanced courses in certain areas, whether he should be encouraged to do independent preparation or other special types of preparation for certain subjects, whether some course other than the regular course is most appropriate for him, or whether he will need remedial instruction in some areas. The University of Chicago has made use of such placements tests for many years (Chicago College Faculty, 1950). The C.E.E.B. (1956) Advanced Placement Program is a step in this same direction as is the new program being planned by the American College Testing organization.

Finally, we still need better tests for the differential prediction of success in the different courses and subject fields. Horst (1959) has been doing some of the pioneering work in this type of prediction. Here the question becomes, not whether the student will succeed or fail in college, but in which subject fields is he likely to do his best work. Such predictions are especially valuable as a basis for guiding and counseling the student about his academic program in college. Although the A.P.S. does help in making differential predictions (see Chapter 3), it is likely that aptitude tests, achievement tests, and other data will be needed for this type of prediction.

Implications for Educational Research

The A.P.S. should become a powerful tool in educational research. Since it gives additional meaning and precision to grades, they may become a more useful source of evidence in educational studies.

The A.P.S. permits the combining of grades from different

schools and colleges and thus enables research workers to pool data obtained from different institutions. Thus, the replication of educational experiments may be carried on more efficiently and accurately. It should also permit the more accurate characterization of the population and school when describing an experiment so that later experiments may be compared with it. With this improvement, discrepancies in results due to differences in the populations studied may be more clearly located.

In educational research in the past we have made great use of scholastic aptitude test scores for matching students in control and experimental populations. It is likely that grades corrected on the basis of the A.P.S. may in the future become one of the important controls in educational experimentation. We may also use grades as one important criterion in determining the effectiveness of the experimental procedure —although the value of tests and other evidence in evaluating the educational outcomes will still be as important as ever because the meaning of the test scores can be more clearly expressed in operational terms than can the meaning of a grade.

As was noted in Chapter 1, a great amount of time and energy has been devoted to the problem of prediction of academic success. The improvement of prediction from $+.50$ to $+.75$ by the use of the A.P.S. suggests that the problem of prediction has been considerably narrowed. There is still room for further improvement in prediction studies, but the variance to be accounted for by new aptitude tests, personality indicators of academic achievement, and other instruments is considerably reduced. Research on over-achievement and under-achievement will be somewhat less significant than hitherto because the proportion of students falling into these classes should be much reduced.

It is likely that much of the effort that has been devoted to the prediction problem will now be increasingly devoted to research on the criterion. What does a grade represent? How can grades be more valid indicators of the achievement of educational objectives? How can grading procedures become more objective and meaningful? How do grading procedures differ from teacher to teacher? How can test results best be combined with teacher judgments in the assignment of grades? These are a few of the questions for which educational research might be profitable.

It is also clear from our data that unless grading is improved we should not expect correlations much higher than those reported here. The correlation of $+.75$ is very close to our estimate of $+.80$ as the reliability of first-year college grade averages. More refined statistical procedures may improve the predictions slightly but major increases in correlation are to be expected only if the reliability of college grades is improved.

However, we must be quick to disclaim any plea for the improvement of college grades merely to improve prediction. College grades are important in their own right as bases for certification, as means of motivating students, and as indices of the achievement of important educational objectives. There is much room for the improvement of grades at both the secondary and college level. The point to be made here is that the development of Academic Prediction Scales high-lights the importance of the criteria of college achievement and leaves relatively little room for research on prediction until the criteria are improved.

Other Problems

We started this study in order to find ways of improving the prediction of college grades. The findings of this study demonstrate that academic prediction can be considerably improved by the use of the students' previous academic records—with suitable modifications. It is clear that the best predictors of grades are grades. The judgments of teachers in college about an individual can be predicted from the judgments made about him by teachers in secondary school. Furthermore, the research of a number of British workers make it clear that the judgments of teachers on a student in secondary school can be predicted from the judgments of teachers about the same student in elementary school.

The development of these improved methods of prediction are of considerable social significance. Academic failure can be reduced. Also, students may be encouraged to secure a higher education by the availability of evidence that they can successfully do work at this level. The methods raise new questions for testing methods, educational research, and grading practices. The results have, however, left us with two problems, problems we would share at least briefly with the reader.

Our first problem is that our methods have enabled us to predict something without quite knowing what it is that we are predicting. College grades can be predicted from high school grades, but what does a grade really mean? If the same teacher assigns B grades to five students in his course in college physics, does this mean that all five students are equal in their competence in physics? We don't really know. One student may have received the B because of creativeness and originality, another because he is so careful and precise in his work, still another may have received the B grade because he has learned what will satisfy the instructor. There may be many different reasons for giving the same grade to different students. In fact, the instructor may vary his criteria in judging the different students.

Furthermore, the same student may receive the same letter grade from different instructors in different courses for different reasons. Put another way, we are saying that different scales may be employed by the same teacher for different students and different scales may be employed by different teachers. There is considerable research showing some of the student characteristics that influence grades. This may include values (Battle, 1954), likeability (Hadley 1954), and other personal qualities.

Grades are complex judgments that can not be defined very precisely. We may talk about an A student and by this mean at least two things. An A student is one whom the teacher judges to be higher in some ways than other students in the same course. We may also mean that an A student is one who attracts A judgments by teachers. That is, he manages to secure such judgements by some means or other.

Someone said that academic prediction was so difficult because grades are "moving targets." We heartily agree with this characterization. The meaning of a grade is a matter which needs to be given more and more attention. Whatever it may mean and however it may change from teacher to teacher and from student to student, grades are relatively consistent for the same individual within a single educational institution and from one institution to the other. Perhaps what needs to be studied is not the teacher and his grades but the "grade getting ability" of the individual student.

Our second problem is very much related to the first. Why are grades so consistent from one level of education to another? The correlation of +.75 reported here is very close to the upper limit of +.80 permitted by the reliability of the criterion. Theoretically we might expect even higher correlations if the reliability of the criterion is increased. Correcting the correlation of +.75 for attenuation (unreliability of our criterion), results in estimates of +.83 to +.94, depending upon what we estimate the reliability of high school grades and college grades to be.* These correlations approach the +.90 found between high school and elementary school achievement by some English workers. Whether we use the +.76 found by Burnham (1959), the +.75 found in this work, the +.83, resulting from our corrections for attenuation, or the +.90 found by the English workers (Yates and Pidgeon, 1957; Pilliner, 1958), the correlations are very high

* Estimating +.80 as the reliability of college and high school grades, $r = +.94$.

  Estimating +.90 as the reliability of college and high school grades, $r = +.83$.

  Estimating +.80 as the reliability of college grades and +.90 as the reliability of high school grades, $r = +.88$.

—so high as to raise serious questions either about the meaning of grades or about the effectiveness of our educational institutions.

If indices of educational achievement are so predictable that fewer than ten individuals out of one hundred differ markedly from the predicted value, it suggests that few individuals shift markedly from the *relative standing* they had previously. It is possible that everyone is developing educationally from one level to another, but there is something disturbing about the vast majority of students maintaining their same relative position as they go from high school to college. The similarity of findings from the elementary to the secondary level and the likelihood of similar findings from the college to the graduate school or professional school (Ward, 1959) suggest a determinism in individual learning patterns. Does the student develop learning patterns or habits very early in his schooling and do these learning patterns remain relatively fixed throughout his academic career? Under what conditions do students really shift in their academic performance? Are some schools more effective than others in changing the learning patterns of their students?

If education is really a challenge to students and different students meet the challenge differently, we might expect less predictability than that reported here. We are not clear why the students' relative level of performance is so predictable, but we believe the problem is one that should be thoroughly investigated. It is related to the report of Jacob (1956) who found little change in attitudes and values as the result of collegiate education. Is this stability the result of early fixing of learning patterns in the individual? Is it the result of a "grade-getting ability" that remains relatively fixed? These are a few of the possible questions that may give meaning to our problem.

In any case we seem bound to seek ways of improving our predictions of human behavior and, when we are successful in this endeavor, we become equally concerned with the attempt to understand why we are able to predict so well.

Appendix on Statistical Procedures

THROUGHOUT THIS WORK WE
have endeavored to use the simplest statistical procedures
because we were convinced that the effect of the scaling procedures was so great that almost any statistical technique
would permit it to emerge. We were also interested in communicating to an audience more interested in the use of the
procedures than in the statistical refinements of the different
methods.

The major statistical technique used in this work is the
regression formula.

$$X_1 = M_1 + r_{12} \frac{\sigma_1}{\sigma_2} (X_2 - M_2)$$

where
$X_1 =$ the corrected scale value.
$X_2 =$ the individual score.
$M_1, M_2 =$ mean value of the two variables.
$r_{12} =$ correlation between the two variables.
$\sigma_1, \sigma_2 =$ the standard deviations of the two variables.

We have used this formula to determine the corrected school or college grades based upon the Internal Method, the corrected school and college grades based upon an aptitude test score (Aptitude Method), and the corrected school and college grades based upon an achievement test battery (Achievement Method).

Throughout this work we have employed only linear correlation and regression techniques. We are of the opinion that the use of non-linear techniques may slightly improve some of the scaling procedures. We would recommend that any organization attempting to improve on our procedures experiment with non-linear techniques. Other more complex statistical procedures such as discriminant analysis and analyses of variance and co-variance are also likely to bring about some refinements over our procedures.

The criterion we have used through this study has been grade averages over the first year of college. It is likely that in some universities significant improvements in prediction will result if scaling procedures are applied to grade averages in particular schools or departments such as Engineering, Liberal Arts, School of Education, etc. Unfortunately, our data did not permit these refinements.

We have explored in only a limited way the possibility of applying scaling procedures to particular subject fields. More must be done to determine the best procedures for scaling grades in particular subject fields.

Although our work has primarily been concerned with the relation between high school grades and college grades, we expect that similar procedures could be applied to under-graduate college grades in relation to professional school and graduate school grades. Similar procedures have been employed by the British workers on the relation between elementary and secondary school grades.

We have not been able to make very elaborate studies of the stability of the scale for a particular school or college over many years. Some of our results indicated considerable stability over one to two years. However, additional research is needed to determine the extent of change in scale values over an extended period of time as well as the explanation for change when it does take place. Ward (1959), studying the stability of grade scales for colleges sending students to the Harvard Business School, found correlations of +.81 for about a five-year period, as contrasted with correlations of +.70 and +.59 for periods up to twelve years. In the early use of grade scales we would urge annual computation of scale values until the reliability of the scales can be determined.

Some of the most thorough research on the scaling of grades and the scaling of teachers' estimates has been done by a number of English workers. The reader will find relatively full statisical treatment of some of the problems in the work of McClelland (1942), Pilliner (1958), and Howard (1958). Yates and Pidgeon (1957) describe the methods they have used in scaling teachers' estimates at the elementary school level.

We have not attempted to explore ways of combining several different scales to produce the maximum correlation. We do believe that some combination of Internal, Aptitude, and Achievement Methods may be superior to any one of them, but regard this as a problem for future research.

What we have attempted to do is determine the effectiveness of several scaling methods as opposed to the use of uncorrected grades. Although we have not reported the significance of the differences between correlations based on uncorrected grades and corrected grades, the differences were so large and so consistent as to leave little question about their utility. For the Internal Method, the correlation of +.77, based on 4,519 cases is significantly different from the +.50 correlation between uncorrected grades at better than the .01% level. Using the cross-validation data on the Internal Method, the correlation of +.72 based on 2,115 cases is significantly different from the +.50 correlation between uncorrected grades at better than the .01% level. For the Aptitude Method, the correlation of +.72 based on 1,827 cases is significantly different from the +.50 correlation between uncorrected grades at better than the .01% level. Thus, the over-all correlations based on grades corrected by the Internal and Aptitude Methods are significantly different from the correlations based on uncorrected grades.

In Tables 10 and 11 of Chapter 3 we have reported correlations for selected high schools and colleges. At both the high school and college levels, using Fisher's Z transformations, the average correlation based on the Internal Method is different from the average correlation based on uncorrected grades at better than the .01% level. At the high school level the average correlation based on the Aptitude Method is different from the average correlation based on uncorrected grades at better than the .01% level. At the college level the average correlation based on the Aptitude Method is not significantly different from the average correlation based on uncorrected grades.

The differences reported here are so large and so consistent as to leave little doubt as to their social as well as statistical significance. We have not tested the significance of the Achievement Method because we are not satisfied that we have made an adequate test of this method for the reasons discussed in Chapter 2.

References

Aikin, W. M. 1942. *The Story of the Eight-Year Study.* New York: Harper.

Anderson, J. E. 1920. "Intelligence Tests of Yale Freshman." *School and Society,* 2 (April 3), 417-20.

Battle, H. 1954. "Application of Inverted Analysis in a Study of the Relation between Values and Achievement in High School Pupils." Unpublished doctoral dissertation, University of Chicago.

Bloom, B. S. 1956. "The 1955 Normative Study of the Tests of General Educational Development." *The School Review,* 64 (March), 110-124.

Burnham, P. S. 1959. "The Assessment of Admission Criteria." *Association of College Admissions Counselors Journal,* 4 (Winter), 1-9.

Chauncey, H. & Frederiksen, N. 1951. "The Functions of Measurement in Educational Placement." *IN* Lindquist, E. F. (Ed.), *Educational Measurement.* Washington: American Council on Education, 85-116.

Chicago College Faculty. 1950. *The Idea and Practice of General Education.* Chicago: University of Chicago Press.

College Board Review, 1959, Spring. No. 38, p. 20.

College Entrance Examination Board. 1956. *Advanced Placement Program.* New York: Author.

Crawford, A. B. & Burnham, P. S. 1946. *Forecasting College Achievement.* New Haven: Yale University Press.

Davenport, K. S. & Remmers, H. H. 1950. "Factors in State Characteristics Related to Average A-12, V-12 Test Scores." *Journal of Educational Psychology,* 41 (February), 110-115.

Dressel, P. L. & Mayhew, L. 1954. *General Education: Explorations in Evaluation.* Washington: American Council on Education.

Dyer, H. S. & King, R. O. 1955. *College Board Scores: Their Use and Interpretation.* New York: College Entrance Examination Board.

Educational Records Bulletin No. 60. 1953. *1952 Fall Testing Program in Independent Schools and Supplementary Studies.* New York: Educational Records Bureau.

Fishman, J. A. 1957. *1957 Supplement to College Board Scores No. 2.* New York: College Entrance Examination Board.

Frederiksen, N. & Schrader, W. B. 1951. *Adjustment to College.* Princeton: Educational Testing Service.

Garrett, H. E. 1947. *Statistics in Psychology and Education.* New York: Longmans, Green.

Guilford, J. P. 1950. *Fundamental Statistics in Psychology and Education.* New York: McGraw-Hill.

Gulliksen, H. 1950. "Criteria for the Evaluation of Achievement Tests from the Point of View of Their External Statistical Relationships." *Proceedings of the 1950 Invitational Conference on Testing Problems.* Princeton: Educational Testing Service.

Hadley, S. T. 1954. "A School Mark: Fact or Fancy?" *Educational Administration and Supervision,* 40 (May), 305-312.

Harris, D. 1940. "Factors Affecting College Grades: A Review of the Literature, 1930-37." *Psychological Bulletin,* 37, 125-166.

Horst, P. 1957. "Differential Prediction in College Admissions." *College Board Review,* No. 33 (Fall) 19-23.

Horst, P. 1959. *Differential Prediction of Academic Success.* Seattle: University of Washington.

Howard, M. 1958. "The Conversion of Scores to a Uniform Scale."
  British Journal of Statistical Psychology, 11 (November), Part
  II, 199-207.
Hungate, T. L. 1957. "To What Extent Will the Local, the State,
  and the Federal Governments Provide Additional Support for
  Institutions of Higher Education?" *Current Issues in Higher
  Education*, 1957, 217-224. Washington: Association for Higher
  Education.
Iffert, R. E. 1956. "Drop-Outs: Nature and Causes; Effects on
  Student, Family, and Society." *Current Issues in Higher
  Education*, 1956. Washington: Association for Higher Educa-
  tion, 94-102.
Jacob, P. E. 1956. *Changing Values in College*. New Haven: Edward
  W. Hazen Foundation.
Jordan, A. M. 1920. "Some Results and Correlations of Army Alpha
  Tests." *School and Society*, 2 (May 20), 354-358.
Jordan, A. M. 1922. "Correlations of Four Intelligence Tests with
  the Grades of Students and with Each Other." *Psychological
  Bulletin*, 19 (February), 93-94.
Learned, W. W. & Wood, B. W. 1938. *The Student and His Knowl-
  edge*. New York: Carnegie Foundation for the Advancement
  of Teaching.
Lincoln, E. A. 1917. "The Relative Standing of Pupils in High
  School, in Early College, and on College Entrance Examina-
  tions." *School and Society*, 5 (April 7), 417-420.
McClelland, W. 1942. *Selection for Secondary Education*. London:
  University of London Press.
McNemar, Q. 1949. *Psychological Statistics*. New York: Wiley.
Muskingum College Faculty. 1937. *A College Looks at Its Program*.
  New Concord, Ohio: Muskingum College.
Odell, C. W. 1927. "Attempt at Predicting Success in Freshman
  Year at College." *School and Society*, 25 (June 11), 702-706.
Pace, R. C. & Stern, G. G. 1958. *A Criterion Study of College
  Environment*. Syracuse: Syracuse University Research Institute,
  Psychological Research Center.
Peters, F. 1952. "The Development of National Scales for High
  School and College Grades." Unpublished master's dissertation,
  University of Chicago.

Pilliner, A. E. G. 1958. "The Rescaling of Teachers' Estimates." *British Journal of Statistical Psychology,* 11 (November), Part II, 191-197.

Reitz, W. 1934. "Predicting College Achievement with Marks and Ranks Adjusted for Inter-High School Variability." *Bulletin of the American Association of College Registrars* (April) 162-181.

Segel, D. 1934. *Prediction of Success in College.* Bulletin No. 15, U. S. Office of Education. Washington: U. S. Government Printing Office.

Stern, G. G., Stein, M. I. & Bloom, B. S. 1956. *Methods in Personality Assessment.* Glencoe, Ill.: The Free Press.

Stuit, D. B. 1949. *Predicting Success in Professional Schools.* Washington: The American Council on Education.

Thurstone, L. L. 1938. *Primary Mental Abilities.* Chicago: University of Chicago Press.

Thurstone, L. L. & Thurstone, T. G. 1938. "The 1937 Psychological Examination for College Freshmen." *Educational Record* (April) 209-234.

Toops, H. A. 1933. "The Transmutation of Marks." *Ohio College Association Bulletin* No. 88 (June 24), 1093-2000. (Mimeo.)

Travers, R. M. W. 1949. "Significant Research on the Prediction of Academic Success." *IN* Donahue, Wilma T.; Coomb, C. H.; & Travers, R. W. *The Measurement of Student Adjustment and Achievement.* Ann Arbor: University of Michigan Press, 147-190.

Walker, H. M. 1943. *Elementary Statistical Methods.* New York: Henry Holt.

Ward, L. B. 1957. "Stable Exchange Rates for Academic Currencies." *College Board Review,* No. 38 (Spring), 26-28.

Wissler, C. 1901. "The Correlation of Mental and Physical Tests." *Psychological Review, Monograph Supplements.* 3 62. New York: Macmillan.

Yates, A. & Pidgeon, D. A. 1957. *Admission to Grammar Schools.* London: Newnes Educational Publishing Co.